THE WORLD OF SCIENCE
WEATHER
AND ITS WORK

THE WORLD OF SCIENCE

WEATHER
AND ITS WORK

DAVID LAMBERT & RALPH HARDY

Facts On File Publications
New York, New York ● Bicester, England

WEATHER AND ITS WORK

Copyright © Macdonald & Co (Publishers) Ltd
1985, 1987

First published in the United States of America in
1984 by Facts on File, Inc., 460 Park Avenue South,
New York, N.Y.10016

First published in Great Britain in 1984 by Orbis
Publishing Limited, London

**Library of Congress Cataloging in Publication
Data**

Main entry under title:

The world of science.

   Includes index.
   Summary: A twenty-five volume encyclopedia of
scientific subjects, designed for eight- to twelve-year-
olds. One volume is entirely devoted to projects.
   1. Science—Dictionaries, Juvenile.   1. Science—
Dictionaries
Q121.J86   1984   500   84-1654

ISBN: 0-87196-987-0

Printed in Yugoslavia
10 9 8 7 6 5 4 3

Previous pages Part of
the tropical coast of
Mexico photographed
from a satellite. As the
temperature increases
during the day,
convection currents
rise to form cumulus
clouds – the little
white blobs in the
picture.

Consultant editors
Eleanor Felder, former managing editor, *New Book of
Knowledge*
James Neujahr, Dean of the School of Education, City
College of New York
Ethan Signer, Professor of Biology, Massachusetts
Institute of Technolgy
J. Tuzo Wilson, Director General, Ontario Science
Centre

Editor Penny Clarke
Designer Roger Kohn

1 WHAT IS WEATHER?

2 WEATHER AROUND THE WORLD

3 WEATHER AT WORK

Note There are some unusual words in this book. They are explained in the Glossary on pages 62–63. The first time each word is used in the text it is printed in *italics*.

◀These palm trees are being lashed by a violent tropical storm on the west coast of Africa. It is not raining yet, but the storm clouds are building up before the downpour starts.

1 WHAT IS WEATHER?

INTRODUCTION

'Lovely weather!' we say when the sun shines brightly . Or, 'Lousy weather!' when it pours with rain. Good or bad weather makes all the difference to holidays and vacations. Weather can also help produce huge crops or spoil a harvest. Rough weather can sink ships. Foggy weather can ground planes. All of us depend on weather more than we may realise.

The world brews weather rather as you make a cake. First, you put flour, sugar, butter and an egg inside a bowl. You might add dried fruit, too. Then you stir your ingredients. Next you cook them in an oven. The kind of cake that comes out depends on three main things: (1) your ingredients; (2) how you mixed them; and (3) the oven temperature and length of cooking.

The main ingredients in weather are air and water in its three different forms: ice, droplets and vapour. Nature's mixing bowl is the earth's ball-shaped outer surface. Cake mixture would fall from a mixing bowl shaped 'inside out' like that. But air cannot fall off the earth because the force of gravity attracts everything, including air, to the earth's surface rather as a magnet attracts iron filings. The sun's heat and the spinning of the earth serve instead of spoons to stir the air about. Lastly, the sun acts as nature's oven, pre-set to cook the air each day for a length of time that depends upon the season. Also the heat from the sun-oven varies from place to place across the world, depending how far each place is from the equator.

The earth is surrounded by the *atmosphere*, which is divided into several layers. The world's weather system is in the *troposphere*, the lower of these layers. Compared with the earth, which is 12,500 km (7,767 miles) across, the troposphere is very thin, varying between 10 and 20 km (6 and 12 miles).

Dust and clouds in the atmosphere absorb or bounce back much of the energy that the sun beams down upon the earth. Less than half that energy gets through to warm the earth's surface and the lower atmosphere. Warmed air combined with the spinning (rotation) of the earth produces winds that spread heat and moisture more evenly around the world. This is very important because the sun heats the equator much more than the poles, and without winds to help restore the balance, much of the earth would be impossible to live on. Where air cools you can get cloud, rain, snow, hail, fog or frost.

The weather that you find in any place depends on many things: how hot and how moist the air is there; how it is being moved by the wind and especially whether it is being lifted or not. It was discovered many years ago that all these factors are related to the air pressure, which is the weight of the atmosphere at any place. The lower the pressure the more likely are rain and strong winds.

All kinds of weather are usually happening at once in different parts of the world. Where you live it might be dull, cool and drizzly. Somewhere else the sun shines hotly from a cloudless sky. A third place could be having a storm. At a fourth place snow is falling. At a fifth place fierce winds may be plucking trees up by their roots. At a sixth place heavy rain may be causing floods. A seventh place is foggy.

Tomorrow, many of these places could be having quite different weather. For weather is what is happening to the atmosphere from hour to hour and day to day.

The next pages show how all the different kinds of weather happen.

HUMIDITY

Humidity is the amount of dampness in the air. All air holds *water vapour*, although it is quite invisible to us. You may have seen drops of water gleaming on grass blades in early morning. Water drops also collect on the inside surface of windows on cold nights. The moisture on the grass and the window comes from water vapour which is made of particles too small to be seen. Air can hold only so much water vapour, but the warmer the air the more it can hold. When air has all the water vapour it can hold the air is said to be *saturated*. If the air is then cooled, any excess water vapour *condenses*. That is, its molecules join to build the water droplets we can see.

The temperature at which this happens is called the *dew point*, which varies according to how much water vapour there is in the air. If air contains a great deal of water vapour dew will form at a temperature of 20°C (68°F). But if the air is rather dry and does not hold much moisture, dew may not form until the temperature drops to 0°C (32°F) or even below freezing.

How dew forms

On clear, cold mornings you may see millions of drops of water sparkling on·

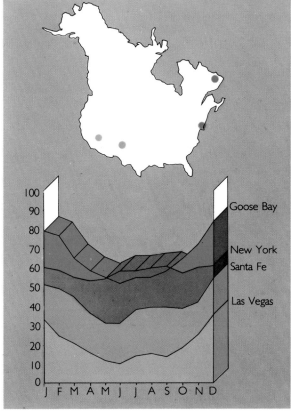

▲Mist shrouds the mountains around Sognefjord, Norway. If mist is so thick that you can see less than 1000m (1100yd) in front of you, meteorologists classify it as fog.

◄This map and diagram show how relative humidity changes during the year at four places in North America. Relative humidity is the amount of water vapour in air compared with the amount needed to saturate that air. Saturated air has a relative humidity of 100%.

lawns, car roofs and wires. These drops are dew. Dew forms when damp air touches objects that cool the air to below its dew point.

What happens goes like this. By day such things as grass blades, window

7

panes and metal surfaces warm up as they receive the sun's heat. They in turn warm the air nearby. So moisture on the ground *evaporates*: it turns to water vapour. But on clear, calm nights the grass, glass and metal lose heat into the clear night sky by *radiation*. As the objects cool they chill nearby air. If this cools to below its dew point, water vapour condenses on the chilly surfaces as dew. Dew forms most readily on objects that easily lose heat, and vegetation like grass which is moist to begin with.

Sometimes warm, moist air moves gently over very cold surfaces. When this happens, cold car windows keep misting over even when wiped clear. Condensation may also form on bathroom walls because the air is fairly warm and very moist and the walls cold by comparison. This moisture is advection dew. You can produce advection dew by breathing on a cold window: water vapour in your warm moist breath condenses on the glass.

Dew forms usually on still, cloudless nights. On windy nights the wind spreads the cooling effect of the ground through a

▼During the night, as the temperature fell, dew formed on this spider's web. But as the temperature gradually rises throughout the morning the dew will evaporate.

deep layer of the atmosphere and so the dew point is not reached. On overcast nights, the clouds help to trap heat near the ground like a giant blanket and temperatures mostly stay above the dew point.

Fog and mist

When a kettle boils, a mass of water droplets we call steam appears to gush from its spout. This is because moisture in hot saturated air from the kettle rapidly condenses in the cooler air outside. Fog is formed rather like this. It is really a cloud on the surface of land or water formed of millions of tiny droplets of water. Land fogs usually form in autumn and winter, when nights are long. On clear, chilly winter nights with very little wind the air just above the ground may cool below its dew point. The coldest heaviest air drains into dips in the ground. Here the air is already saturated with moisture evaporated from rivers, lakes and plants. So fog first fills valleys. Light winds then spread the cooling effect, so more air reaches its dew point and fog becomes more widespread. This is radiation fog.

Fog also forms when fairly warm, moist air crosses a cold surface. This is called advection fog.

Sea fogs mostly happen when warm air blows over a cold ocean current. In a similar way fogs also form inland over frozen lakes or snow.

Sometimes cold air moves across water that is at a higher temperature. The cold air mixes with the very shallow layer of warmer moist air near the surface. This cools to below its dew point and a wispy fog forms. It is called arctic sea smoke because it looks like smoke rising from the water. It only happens in cold weather.

Fogs are seldom very deep. Sea fogs can lie so low that ships' masts poke out above them.

Sometimes when temperatures are below freezing, fog droplets freeze on anything they touch. This is what is called *freezing fog*. Sometimes the frost remains long after the fog has cleared.

Mist is similar to fog but thinner, because it has fewer water droplets.

◄Moisture-loving ferns and lichens grow thickly on these tree branches in clean, humid air. Unlike most plants, these ferns suck moisture from damp air instead of from damp soil. Plants that grow on other plants like this are epiphytes.

▲Clouds tower over the Andes Mountains in Peru. Some clouds develop here as warm air cools when it rises to cross the mountains. Clouds also form as lower slopes warm the air above so that it rises, then cools.

CLOUDS

Sometimes clouds drift like gleaming blobs of cotton wool across a bright blue sky. At other times a drab grey sheet of cloud may hide the sun or stars. If you fly above these clouds by day their tops are bright with reflected sunlight. But if your plane climbs or dives through a cloud you seem to plunge into a dull, grey clammy fog. This is hardly surprising, for most clouds are made of the same ingredients as fog. The main difference is that clouds form high above the level of low-lying ground.

How clouds grow

The water droplets in a cloud come from water vapour that has evaporated from the sea or moist surfaces on land. Water vapour is a gas made up of water molecules, the tiniest particles of water that there are. These molecules move about among the molecules that make up air. When air grows warm, molecules of air and water move more rapidly and spread far apart. This thinning out makes warm air and its water vapour light enough to rise through the cooler air.

But air grows cooler as it rises. Its temperature drops 1°C for every 100 m (1.8°F for every 300 ft) that the air floats upward. So air that had a temperature of 27°C (80°F) at sea level has cooled to 12°C (54°F) when it has risen 1500 m (4920 ft).

As the rising air cools, it can hold less moisture than before. When the air cools to its dew point its invisible water vapour starts condensing into water droplets to form a cloud.

Warm air only rises to form a cloud if the air above it is cool. If the air above is also warm it stops the warm, lower air rising.

Condensation particles

Clouds form as water molecules condense on solid particles already in the air. Billions of tiny particles are drifting in the air around us. As they blow, the winds pick up minute grains of salt from sea spray, or specks of dust and pollen from the land. Clouds appear as moist air rises to a level where its water vapour starts condensing on such particles. This is called the condensation level. Its height depends largely on the amount of moisture in the rising air. Air that was almost saturated with water vapour before it started rising may reach its condensation level a few hundred metres above the ground. But air with very little moisture may float up as high as 11 km (6.8 miles) before clouds start to form.

If moist air rises very high indeed its water molecules form ice crystals. Some clouds are made entirely of ice.

6

5

4

3

Six photographs of a thundercloud in the making. **1, 2** The cloud grows as updraughts of warm air carry water vapour to heights of 16 km (10 miles) or more. **3** The rising vapour cools and condenses into water and ice crystals.
4, 5 Some 12 km (7.5 miles) up, strong winds of the upper air drag the cloud crest sideways.
6 This makes the cloud look like a giant anvil.

2

1

11

CLOUD TYPES

Clouds come in many shapes and sizes. Different kinds occur with different types of weather. *Meteorologists* (weather scientists) describe clouds by their shape and general appearance. The three main types are heaped, layered and feathery. Heaped clouds build upwards, and are usually taller than they are wide. Layered clouds spread out like a sheet which can be hundreds of kilometres across. Feathery clouds are wispy streaks, often curling at one end. They are always very high and made up of ice crystals. Weathermen describe heaped clouds as *cumuliform* from the Latin word *cumulus* which means 'heap'. They call layered clouds *stratiform* from the Latin *stratum*, meaning 'spread'. Feathery clouds get their name from *cirrus*, the Latin for a 'curl of hair'.

Heaped clouds build where warm, moist air is rising fast like huge bubbles. Some are fine-weather clouds but the largest bring thunderstorms. Layered clouds form mostly when warm air is slowly lifted, often as it moves over a region of colder air lying at a lower level. When deep enough they can bring spells of rain, drizzle or snow. Some feathery clouds are pulled out into long plumes with a hooked end. Such clouds often hint at unsettled weather on the way.

Weathermen list 10 main kinds of cloud. Some have names made by joining two of the three Latin names just mentioned. Other names include *alto* meaning 'high' or *nimbus* meaning 'rain'. Each name, then, holds clues to a cloud's shape or height or the weather that comes with it.

Weathermen often group these 10 types of cloud according to their height, as low, medium or high cloud. Cloud types with a low base are cumulus, cumulonimbus, nimbostratus, stratus and stratocumulus. Stratocumulus clouds are really a mixture of layer and heap clouds. The two medium-level cloud forms are altocumulus and altostratus. The three forms of high clouds are cirrus, cirrocumulus and cirrostratus.

►Altocumulus is a thin, fleecy type of cloud. Its globe-shaped patches often form long bands with blue sky between. Altocumulus is a medium-level type of cloud seen usually in fine, settled weather.

►Stratocumulus is a low cloud made of rolls or ball-shaped masses. These tend to join to form a low cloud layer. From below, this cloud looks dull and grey. From above, it forms a shining sea of fluffy white.

►Nimbostratus cloud is dark grey and sheds drizzly rain in summer and snow in winter. This low layered cloud forms below 2000 m (6600 ft). In the photograph, the front edge of a nimbostratus cloud layer has begun to cover the sky.

►Cumulonimbus cloud is heavy and dark and towers high into the sky. Its top can rise 4600 m (15,000 ft) above its base. The top often spreads and flattens. This kind of cloud brews thunderstorms.

◄Cirrus cloud is wispy cloud that forms high up, where air is so cold that the cloud's moisture is frozen as icy crystals. Cirrus often appears in fine weather. But if a high, milky layer of cirrostratus follows, there may be rain.

RAIN

A shower that drenches you and spoils your picnic also soaks the soil and so might save a farmer's thirsty crops. We may not enjoy rain very much but most living things depend upon it for the moisture that they need.

Why rain falls

The rain you see falling from a cloud originally came from water that evaporated from seas, lakes, rivers, moist land surfaces and vegetation.

Billions of droplets and minute ice crystals go to build even the smallest cloud. In a 'warm' cloud, where the temperature is above freezing, droplets of different sizes may collide and merge together. Eventually they become too big and heavy to float in the air. Drizzle can form in this way, but large raindrops form by a more complicated process. In cold clouds containing both water droplets and ice crystals water will condense onto ice crystals and evaporate from droplets at the same time. This means that ice crystals grow quickly and start falling through the cloud collecting any other droplets and smaller crystals in their path. Eventually they reach the ground as rain drops or snow flakes.

Hail forms only when strong up-currents of air carry partly melted ice crystals back high into a cold cloud. These crystals collect layers of ice from colliding with many smaller drops.

Rain water is never absolutely pure. It dissolves gases from the air as it falls. This makes it slightly acid, especially downwind of industrial areas. Sometimes it collects dust suspended in the air, causing muddy deposits where it falls.

Amounts of rainfall

Small raindrops less than 0.5 mm (0.02 in) across often take an hour or more to reach the ground. Light rain like this is known as drizzle. It usually falls from layered cloud less than 2 km (1.2 miles) thick. A heavy, sudden shower of large raindrops or hail falls from a heaped cumulonimbus cloud which might be 15 km (9 miles) or more deep.

Weathermen measure the amount of rain that falls as the depth of water which they collect in devices called rain gauges. They describe rain as light, moderate or heavy. Light rain is rain falling at less than 0.5 mm (0.02 in) per hour. Moderate rain is rain falling at 0.5 to 4 mm (0.02 to 0.16 in) per hour. Heavy rain is rain falling at the rate of more than 4 mm (0.16 in) per hour. Cilaos, an island in the Indian Ocean, once had 1870 mm (74 in) of rain in only 24 hours.

Types of rainfall

Rain can form in three main ways.

Where the sun's heat warms sea or land, warm, moist air may rise high in the sky. As this air spreads and cools, cumulus or cumulonimbus clouds form. These are called convection clouds and the thunderstorms and showers they bring are often called convectional rain. Rain like this falls all the year round near the equator. Away from the equator, convectional rain falls overland mostly in the warmer months. Although when cold

▼Billions of water drops built these towering clouds. Long streaks hanging from the main cloud bank are showers of rain. If the air below is very hot, the rain might all evaporate before it hits the ground. This scene is in east Africa, where rain falls from clouds that picked up moisture as they blew in from the Indian Ocean.

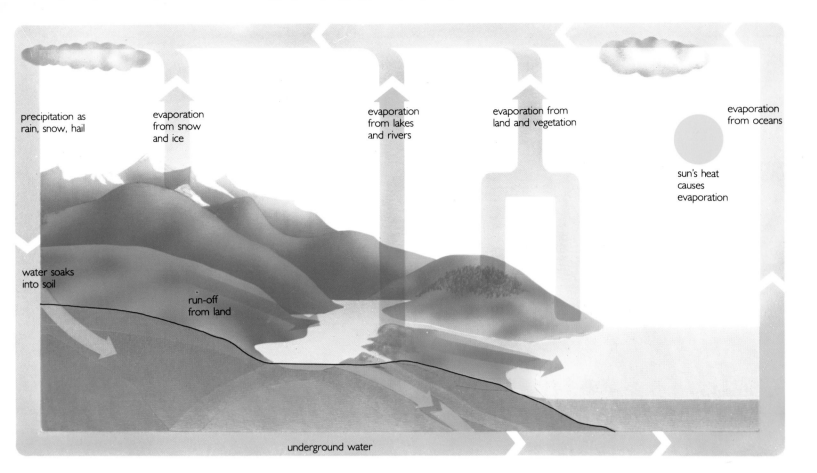

precipitation as
rain, snow, hail

evaporation
from snow
and ice

evaporation
from lakes
and rivers

evaporation from
land and vegetation

evaporation
from oceans

sun's heat
causes
evaporation

water soaks
into soil

run-off
from land

underground water

air flows over relatively warm seas, showers are frequent in winter.

When moist sea air, especially from the great oceans, reaches mountains these may receive *relief rainfall*. The air picks up moisture as it blows across the sea. When it reaches land the moist air had to rise to cross the mountains. The rising air cools and sheds rain on the mountains' coastal slopes. The air sheds so much moisture here that it is much drier when it descends the far side of the mountains. So this side has a drier climate.

The most important source of rain in many parts of the world is frontal rain, which may affect many thousands of square kilometres in a single day. Winds over the earth tend to transfer heat from the tropics towards the poles, and in the middle latitudes encounter cold winds from arctic regions returning towards the equator. The zone where these air masses meet is known as the *polar front*. Low pressure systems, or *depressions*, often occur along this front, as the warm, moist tropical air is gradually forced to rise above the cold air it is drawn into the depression. Then the spirals of cloud that you see on satellite pictures form, often giving large areas of steady rain before the depression fills and the clouds disperse.

▲The sun's heat makes moisture evaporate from all kinds of surfaces, but mostly from oceans. Water vapour condenses to form rain, hail or snow that falls to earth again. There most fallen water runs off the land or soaks into the soil. Either way much water returns to the sea. Water is always travelling from the earth's surface up into the air and back. This round-and-around journey is called the water cycle.

▼A heavy shower blurs the shapes of trees and forms pools of water on the ground. Here, in northern Nigeria, such showers are frequent in the summer months. After each heavy shower may come light rain for an hour or so.

THUNDERSTORMS

Anyone caught out in a thunderstorm is never likely to forget it. Rain and maybe *hail* cascade from a huge, inky cloud. Brilliant flashes of lightning streak between the cloud and the ground. Each flash is followed by the thump of thunder. The bangs and flashes can be as terrifying as gunfire on a battlefield.

What is lightning?

Lightning is a giant electric spark that leaps from cloud to ground or from cloud to cloud. No one knows for certain just what happens, but lightning might occur like this. In a thunderstorm, draughts of warm, moist air rush up inside a thundercloud – the kind meteorologists call a cumulonimbus cloud. On a humid summer day, hot air may quickly climb 10,000 m (32,800 ft). Moisture in the rising air condenses to form billions of water drops and ice crystals. These pick up tiny electric charges as they move through the air, but the amount they pick up depends on their size and shape. The violent air currents in thunder clouds move different sized particles at different speeds. So particles of similar size and with similar amounts of electricity become concentrated in the same part of the cloud. Usually a very high positive electrical charge is formed in the cold higher parts, while near the ground the thundercloud is usually negatively charged.

The big difference between the charges at the top and bottom creates a powerful voltage or electric pressure. This 'push' sends a flash of lightning streaking through the cloud between those parts with opposite electric charges. This is called sheet lightning because from the ground it seems to cover a large area. This is because it is reflected by the clouds. The more violent the updraughts and downdraughts in the thundercloud the greater the electric charges that build up, and the more powerful the lightning they produce.

The bottom of a thundercloud builds up a very powerful negative charge, while the earth below the cloud is normally positively charged. This difference in

▲ A brilliant flash of lightning brightens the night sky above a sea. A leader stroke darts down in quick jumps as it seeks the easiest path to the sea.
Branches of lightning streak out to both sides of the leader, but fizzle out. An instant after the main leader hits the sea a powerful return stroke jumps back up, too fast for you to be able to tell them apart.

charges often creates a voltage powerful enough for a giant spark to flash between the cloud and ground. This is called forked lightning because you can often see two or more paths of lightning. For that to happen the voltage must be very great indeed; dry air resists the flow of electricity so strongly that you would need 30,000 volts to produce a spark across a dry-air gap measuring only 1 cm (2.54 in). That is more than 100 times the voltage of your home's electricity supply. Many lightning flashes exceed one million volts.

A lightning flash always takes the easiest path to earth. It zigzags downward in the wettest regions of the air, because it travels more easily through moist air. The downstroke blasts a kind of invisible channel through the air to the ground. Almost instantly, a return stroke leaves the ground and flashes up by the same channel.

Risks from lightning

You are not very likely to be struck by lightning unless you happen to be on an open hilltop in the middle of a storm. But as lightning can kill or badly burn people, animals and trees, it is best to be careful. Never shelter under isolated trees that are probable targets for lightning.

You are perfectly safe in a car because lightning will travel around the outside of it, if the car is struck. You are usually safe indoors, as most old houses have seen thousands of thunderstorms, but it may be wise to unplug aerials and electrical equipment.

Thunder

The loud bang of thunder happens when lightning tears a path through air. The intense heat produced by lightning makes the nearby particles of air suddenly spread out. The heated particles collide with others that bang against *their* neighbours. In this way a wave of sound energy speeds out from the lightning stroke.

You hear thunder only after you have seen a flash of lightning. This is because sound travels much more slowly than light. Sound travels at about 330 m (1100 ft) per second, while light (and radio waves) travel at *300,000 km (186,000 miles) per second.* Counting how many seconds separate a flash of lightning from a clap of thunder tells you roughly how far away a lightning flash occurred. A gap of 10 seconds means that the lightning struck about 3 km (about 2 miles) away.

▲ The sky darkens and a rising wind stirs tree branches as a thundercloud arrives. Fierce updraughts of air lift moisture high inside the cloud and cold downdraughts drag the moisture down again. These violent actions produce heavy rain or hail. The rising and falling of ice pellets and water drops produces lightning, too.

FREEZING

▲Hoar frost and a sprinkling of snow cover the bare twigs of trees by an English lane. Hoar frost forms when water vapour turns directly to ice without first condensing into water droplets. Hoar frost is made of millions of tiny needle-shaped crystals. Each juts out from the surface on which it formed.

In cold weather water loses enough heat to freeze solid. Frozen water produces the sheets of ice that cover winter ponds. Ice, frost, hail and snow are all frozen moisture, they are just formed in different ways.

Frost

On a long, clear night, the ground and air near the ground may cool below 0°C (32°F). This is the temperature at which fresh water usually freezes. If the air is moist, water vapour from the air may first condense as dew drops on solid objects. Then the dew drops freeze. But if the dew point is below freezing, water vapour turns directly into small, needle-shaped ice crystals. These coat leaves and fences in what looks like thin, white, sparkling fur. This kind of ice is *hoar frost*. The crust of ice that grows on twigs and branches in a freezing fog is another kind of frost, called *rime*. Indoors, water may condense as dew on windowpanes. If

these grow cold enough, ice crystals spread through the water drops one by one, and the mass of small drops freezes to form lovely shapes like ferns or feathers. This kind of ice is sometimes called fern frost.

Hail

Hail is small lumps of ice that fall from thunderclouds. Most hailstones are round or roughly pear-shaped and no larger than a pea. But a few are much bigger. The largest known hailstone was said to be almost as large as a man's head and as heavy as a melon. This monster fell in the American state of Kansas in 1970.

Hailstones are born when water droplets freeze into small ice crystals in a thundercloud. Strong air currents whirl the crystals up and down between cold and warmer parts of the cloud. Each time a crystal falls, water droplets in the lower cloud freeze onto it. Each time it is lifted up, smaller crystals stick to its wet surface. In this way a hailstone gains several coats of ice, growing larger and larger with layers like an onion. A hailstone might be whisked up and down for as long as an hour before it grows too heavy to remain up in the cloud.

Hail usually falls in short, sharp showers called hailstorms. Most only last a few minutes, but that can be enough to cause great damage. Hailstones can flatten fields of grain and strip leaves from grape vines. They can also smash greenhouse windows by the hundred.

Snow

Snow is made up of billions of tiny ice crystals, usually clustered together as snow flakes, that fall from cold clouds. The crystals first form when a rising cloud becomes saturated and the water vapour freezes directly onto dust particles. This only happens when the air is very cold, usually below −20°C (−4°F), well below the usual freezing temperature of water. The first tiny crystals grow as more ice is deposited on them. All snow crystals have six sides, yet no two crystals appear exactly alike. Some are flat, others look like needles.

Their shapes depend on the amount of moisture in the air and on the temperature.

Very cold crystals fall as fine, powdery snow, but at temperatures just above freezing snow crystals stick together and fall as large, fluffy snowflakes. Wet snow like this is best for making snowballs. The large snowflakes drift down more slowly than the smallest, lightest raindrops. In fact, most rain starts off in the clouds as snow but melts before it reaches the ground.

When water falls as snow it forms a much deeper layer than if it falls as rain. For example, a layer of very cold snow may lie 36 times as deep as the same amount of rainwater. This is because air gaps take up so much of the space in fallen snow. As much as 4.8 m (15 ft 9 in) of snow once fell in one tremendous snowstorm on Mt Shasta, California, and near the Great Lakes of North America falls of 1 m (3 ft 3 in) or more are quite common.

Snow may fall even if the air temperature is a few degrees above freezing, but the snow is wet and will melt on the ground. However, heavy or prolonged snow will cool the air enough to stay frozen. Sometimes in winter rain will gradually turn to snow as the air cools. Rain and snow falling together is called sleet.

▼Icicles form when water freezes as it drips off roofs and trees. This often happens in clear winter weather. By day the sun's warmth melts some snow. At dusk the meltwater freezes drip by drip. By dawn long rods of ice have grown down from the eaves of buildings.

▲Deep snow covers the surface of most of Antarctica, the world's coldest continent. Here, snow never melts but piles up year on year. The weight of snow on top crushes snow below until this turns to ice. Much of Antarctica wears a layer of ice and snow many kilometres thick.

THE WIND

▲The invisible wind drives racing yachts over the sea. Before ships had engines, sailors relied on the wind to shift people and cargoes across oceans. Captains learnt to hitch rides on the strong, steady winds that always blow over parts of the world.

You can feel wind on your skin and see twigs moved by the wind. Yet you cannot *see* the wind, for wind is simply moving air. There are small, local winds, like those blowing round the corner of a house or up or down a valley, and vast winds that belong to moving air masses thousands of kilometres across.

All winds are named after the direction they are blowing from. Thus a north wind blows from the north, a south wind from the south, and so on. Changing wind direction often brings a change in weather. In the *northern hemisphere*, you often find that a south or west wind brings warm or mild wet weather, while a north or east wind brings colder, drier weather, especially in the winter.

The great wind systems

Much of the world's weather depends on a great system of winds that blow in set directions. This pattern depends in turn upon the different amounts of sunshine that the different regions of the world receive, and also on the spin of the earth. Above hot surfaces air expands because the air molecules spread out. Above cold surfaces the air molecules are much more closely packed together. Thus hot air is less dense and heavy than the same amount of cold air at the same level and so it rises. It is this difference of density and pressure over continents and oceans, and between hot and cold regions, that sets winds blowing.

Above the hot tropical regions the air expands and rises. On the surface of the land, or sea, only light breezes blow. They often change direction and are known as the Doldrums. This was a dangerous area for the great sailing ships of past centuries. There was so little wind, they were often becalmed for weeks. High up, the rising air flows north and south, gradually cooling and sinking as it grows denser. This happens at about 20° to 30° latitude north and south of the equator in regions known as the sub-tropics. Here the pressure is high and the weather usually fine. Most of the world's deserts are in these latitudes. Sailors called these belts of calm high pressure air around the world the Horse Latitudes. This is because horses sometimes died of thirst here when the sailing ships that carried them were becalmed.

From the sub-tropics air near the earth's surface tends to move in two directions. Some flows back towards the equator to fill the 'gap' left by air rising in the Doldrums. Warm air blowing towards the equator like this creates the steady north-easterly or south-easterly *Trade Winds*. Meanwhile, some warm air from the sub-tropics flows north towards the polar regions.

Cold, dense air covers chilly polar lands and seas. This high-pressure air blows outwards towards the sub-tropics. Cold polar air and warm sub-tropical air meet and clash in the middle latitudes, from

►Strong wind has a harmful effect on plants: it dries out the leaves and distorts the plant's growth. This yew tree is exposed to constant westerly winds from the sea which have stopped new growth on the windward side.

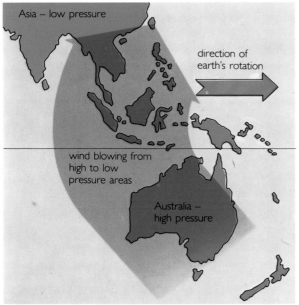

about 30° to 70° north or south of the equator. These are regions of often unsettled weather called the zones of changeable Westerlies.

If the world kept still instead of turning, the winds would tend to blow due north or south. But the earth's spin steers them to one side. This is to the right for winds blowing in the northern hemisphere, and to the left for winds in the southern hemisphere. Trade Winds and Polar Easterlies curve westward as they head for the equator, while the winds between, the Westerlies, curve eastward as they head towards the poles.

▲The earth's rotation steers winds as they cross the equator (the thin black line). The broad arrow shows what happens to a south-east wind blowing from Australia towards low-pressure air over Asia. The rotating earth steers the wind eastward. So as it crosses the equator, the wind blows from the south, then from the south-west.

►This photograph shows the huge dust cloud produced when volcanic Mt Vesuvius erupted in 1944. A long plume of cloud shows where high-level winds drag dust away to the east. When a big volcanic eruption happens, winds high in the atmosphere can carry dust particles right around the world.

CYCLONES AND ANTICYCLONES

▲This whirling white pinwheel of clouds is an intensely strong low-pressure system. Winds blow the clouds around its centre, where air pressure is lowest. *Apollo 7*'s crew took this photograph while their spacecraft was in orbit over the earth.

If winds always blew as described on page 20, the weather would not vary much throughout the year. But changing seasons, day and night, and the positions of land and sea affect the way winds blow from time to time and place to place.

Land and sea breezes

In warm weather, land warms up faster than sea. In cold weather, sea cools down more slowly than land. This sets up pressure differences in the air above land and sea. A summer's day beside the sea is enough to show how changing temperatures affect the wind. In the morning, the land soon becomes warmer than the sea, so a sea breeze blows onshore to replace warm air that rises from the land. In the evening, the sea is warmer than the land which cools rapidly, so now a land breeze blows offshore to replace the warm air rising

over water.

On a far larger scale, this happens over continents and oceans. For instance in winter, the dense, high-pressure air over chilly continents tries to flow out to replace warm, low-pressure air rising from nearby oceans. The earth's rotation steers such winds aside. In the northern hemisphere, winds tend to blow counterclockwise around areas of low pressure called *cyclones* or depressions. But winds blow clockwise around high-pressure air masses, called *anticyclones*. In the southern hemisphere, these wind directions are reversed.

As the seasons change, the major wind systems in some parts of the world do too. This happens especially in places with a monsoon climate where, after months of dry weather, there may be weeks of torrential rain (see page 40).

Stormy and settled weather

Winds are mostly light in the air masses of anticyclones. In mid-latitudes, anticyclones tend to bring hot, sunny weather in summer, and cold, cloudless frosty weather in winter. But cyclones bring windy weather with periods of rain or snow. The largest depressions appear in mid-latitudes where warm Westerlies meet with cold air from the Polar Easterlies. This happens along the polar front, the shifting boundary between sub-tropical and polar air.

First a bulge of warm air juts out into the colder denser air producing a small area of low pressure and rising air. The winds high above may encourage the air

▶Heavy showers fall from storm clouds like this. The showers form where cold fronts force warm, moist air to rise fast and high.

to rise, bringing more warm air into the low-level circulation. This makes the depression deepen even more, until eventually it covers a very large area with very strong winds. The spirals of cloud you see in satellite pictures form in the depression because the warm, moist air rides up above the cold air. The clouds form and give rain or snow.

Most depressions track from west to east across the oceans of mid-latitudes and some measure thousands of kilometres across. Many last several days. When all the warm air has risen and cold winds have blown in to take its place, the strong winds and rains die out. Then, meteorologists say the depression has filled.

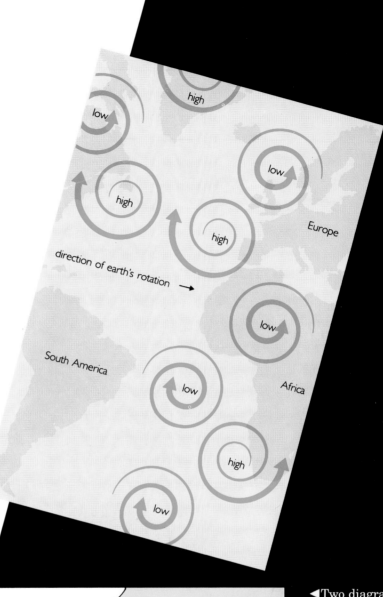

▶Winds blow in different directions around high- and low-pressure systems. Which way the wind blows depends on whether there is a high- or low-pressure system overhead and whether it is in the northern or southern half of the world. Wind direction changes as a pressure system moves overhead from west to east. In a low-pressure system the strongest winds blow near the centre. In a high-pressure system the strongest winds blow around the edges.

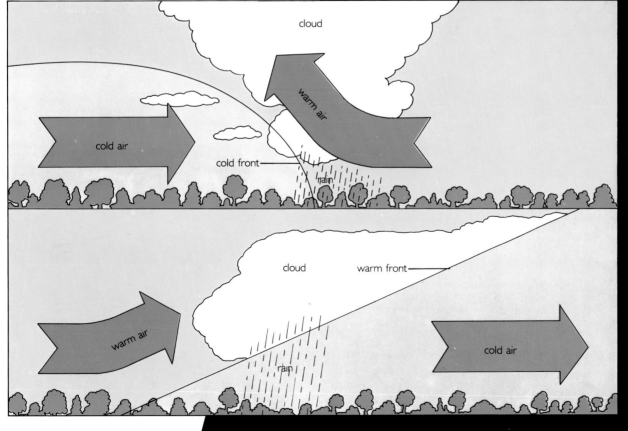

◀Two diagrams show weather where cold and warm air meet in a depression.
Below left: A warm front forms where warm air slides up and over cold air. Warm fronts bring rain or drizzle.
Left: A cold front forms as cold air undercuts the warm air from behind. Cold fronts bring scattered clouds with heavy showers and sunny periods.

HURRICANES AND TORNADOES

►Fierce winds lash palm trees and hurl sand and spray inland. At their strongest, hurricane winds blow at more than 320 km (200 miles) per hour.

▼This diagram shows a hurricane as if sliced down through the middle. Notice the corridors of cloud that whirl around its calm centre, the eye of the hurricane. Arrows are trade winds pulled in towards the eye. The earth's rotation makes winds spiral anticlockwise around hurricanes in the northern hemisphere, but clockwise around those in the southern hemisphere.

Two kinds of low-pressure systems produce the world's fiercest winds. These low-pressure systems are hurricanes and tornadoes.

Hurricanes
Hurricanes are tropical storms so fierce that they can sink ships and smash houses. They get their name from a West Indian word meaning 'big wind'. Hurricanes have other names in other regions. In the south China Sea people call them typhoons, probably from Chinese words meaning 'wind which strikes'. Off north-west Australia, hurricanes are 'willy-willies'. In the Indian Ocean people call them cyclones, although that name can also mean depressions (see pages 22–23).

Hurricanes develop in tropical oceans on both sides of the equator. In summer and autumn, tropical sea water grows

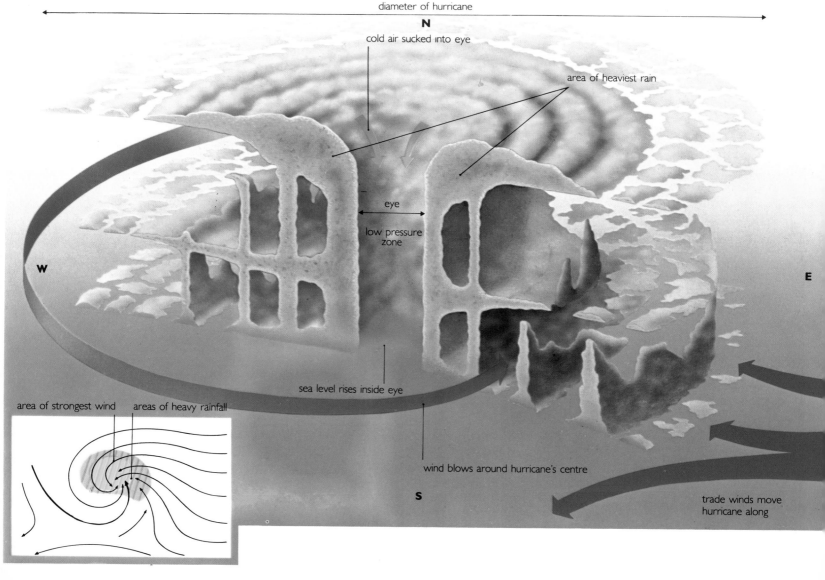

diameter of hurricane

N

cold air sucked into eye

area of heaviest rain

eye

low pressure zone

W

E

sea level rises inside eye

area of strongest wind   areas of heavy rainfall

wind blows around hurricane's centre

S

trade winds move hurricane along

very warm and much moisture evaporates. Very moist updraughts of air, called convection currents, rise through the atmosphere. Occasionally they meet very strong high-level winds which encourage further convection currents, so air rushes in to replace the rising air. Banks of cloud are formed around a calm clear 'eye' by the spiralling wind. This is a hurricane. Torrential rain falls, but it is the wind that causes most damage. Winds scream around the hurricane centre at 110 km per hour (74 mph) or more. Some even rage at twice that speed. The area of violent winds is usually about 25 km (16 miles) across.

At sea, hurricanes whip up mighty waves. On land, the fierce winds uproot trees and flatten flimsy buildings. Winds also send sea sweeping over low-lying countryside. In the worst ones thousands of people may be drowned. The worst-hit coasts lie on the Caribbean Sea, the Gulf of Mexico, the Indian Ocean, the south China Sea, and the Timor Sea off north-west Australia. But the country inland usually escapes, because no hurricane lasts long away from its power supply – the sea.

A hurricane can travel thousands of kilometres and last a week or more although it may move no faster than you can cycle. Winds usually push hurricanes west. Then they curve away from the equator and may head east before they peter out, or become a much less violent but larger depression.

Tornadoes

The fiercest winds of all are those in a tornado. Tornadoes are whirling funnels of air that seem to hang down from a black thundercloud. Because tornadoes writhe like snakes, people also call these whirlwinds 'twisters'. The very largest twister is only 500 m (1600 ft) across where it touches the ground, and most are much less, so they are only about a hundredth of the size of a hurricane. A tornado's winds sometimes swoop around its centre at over 320 km per hour (200 mph). So tornadoes can inflict savage damage on objects in their path. They can pluck up people, animals and cars, and uproot trees. Even heavy objects can be

whirled high above the ground and dropped far from their starting place. But the worst damage can come from the calm 'eye' inside the funnel. The air inside the eye is less dense than the air outside, and the pressure is much lower. So, as a tornado moves quickly across a house, the denser air inside the house presses out far harder than air outside presses in. When this happens to a flimsy building the air inside bursts out and the building explodes as if a bomb had hit it.

Many countries suffer from tornadoes. In the United States hundreds happen in the Mississippi Valley every spring and summer. These form where warm, moist low-lying air from the Gulf of Mexico to the south meets colder, drier high-level air from the Rocky Mountains to the north-west.

Tornadoes that develop over water are called waterspouts. They suck up a cone of water instead of dust, cars and trees. Tornadoes and waterspouts both usually last only half an hour or so.

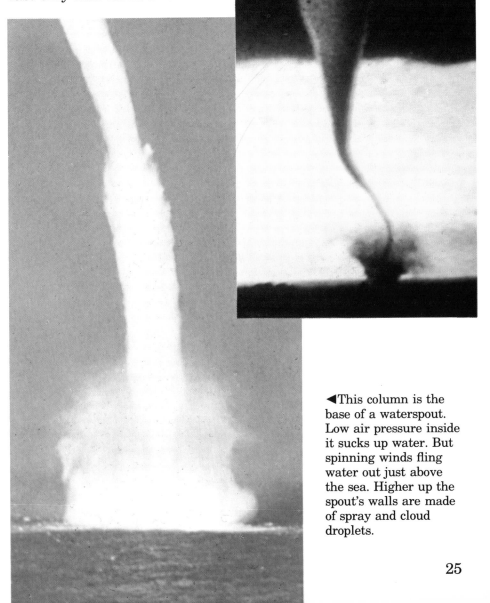

▼This narrow, funnel-shaped cloud hanging from the thundercloud is a tornado. Where the funnel touches the ground fierce winds whirl aloft objects large and small. Wreckage follows its path.

◄This column is the base of a waterspout. Low air pressure inside it sucks up water. But spinning winds fling water out just above the sea. Higher up the spout's walls are made of spray and cloud droplets.

DROUGHTS AND FLOODS

From time to time the weather behaves like a machine gone wildly wrong. For months no rain falls, or perhaps it pours in torrents. Of course some places are usually rainier than others. But almost anywhere can be unusually wet or – even outside deserts – astonishingly dry.

Droughts

Long periods with no snow or rain are known as droughts. Droughts are caused by very long-lasting anticyclones. This is because the air in anticyclones sinks and warms up dissolving cloud instead of rising and cooling to build rain-shedding clouds. Fog may form but no rain falls to replace moisture that sinks into the ground or evaporates. Shallow pools dry up and soil becomes dusty or rock hard. Because they cannot suck up moisture, short-rooted plants turn brown and die. Then grazing animals begin to starve.

Certain places suffer more from droughts than others. Long droughts are rare in fairly rainy countries like the British Isles. At least some rain or snow has fallen there in every month since 1855. But in some countries hardly any

▲The far-off bridge shows that this 'desert' is really the dried-up bed of a broad river. Drought has left only puddles where people wash clothes and drink. Many die, for the drought killed their crops and they have little food left. This drought occurred in India.

▼In long droughts, mud dries up and shrinks. Cracks split its surface to form 'crazy paving'. Clay cracks like this when drought dries up shallow pools and exposes the mud on the bottom.

rain may fall for years. This often happens in parts of India, China and Africa. In the 1930s drought completely killed plants in the prairies of the American Midwest. There were no plant roots to hold the earth together, and the topsoil became loose and blew away from farms in states like Oklahoma. From 1930 to 1940 land that had once grown great crops of grain became like a desert. It was nicknamed the Great Dust Bowl. In the mid-1970s drought gripped the Sahel, a great strip of Africa just south of the Sahara Desert. Herds of cattle and thousands of people died of thirst and hunger. In the early 1980s farmers slaughtered thousands of sheep already dying from Australia's worst drought in many years. Meanwhile crops failed year after year in rainless parts of southern Spain.

Droughts in middle latitudes often happen when a large area of high pressure gets 'stuck' so that depressions bringing rain are steered to the north or south. These are called 'blocking' anticyclones, because they block the paths of depressions. They cause the hottest summers and coldest winters, as well as droughts.

Floods

Flooding happens when rivers overflow because they cannot carry all the water running off the land's surface. The floodwater may be just enough to make riverside meadows squelchy, or it might rise high and fast enough to wash away bridges, roads and cars, and destroy houses. Floods can also occur where very high tides, perhaps helped by strong winds, break through or overflow sea walls.

Floods often happen when depressions, hurricanes or thunderstorms shed unusually large amounts of rain over a short period, especially when rivers are high and the ground very wet. A heavy burst of rain can be too much for the normal drainage and cause the sudden overflowing called a *flash flood*. In 1975 a flash flood struck part of London. Cars floated down the city streets and subways

filled with water. In 1976 a flash flood surged through Big Thompson Canyon in Colorado. The seething waters drowned 80 people, smashed a road and flattened a broad belt of forest.

Flooding also follows weeks of heavy, steady rain. After a rainy autumn in 1966 the River Arno overflowed, drowning streets and churches in the Italian city of Florence. Many fine old paintings were damaged or destroyed. But some of the worst flood disasters of this kind hit the river plains of India and China.

Low coasts in India and Bangladesh also suffer flooding when fierce winds, often in hurricanes out to sea, heap up the surface of the sea and send waves surging far inland. In 1970 about one million Bangladeshis drowned when floods swamped islands in the River Ganges.

In spring melting snow can cause floods, often when the weather suddenly turns mild and wet. From time to time, meltwater has overflowed the United States' Mississippi river system, turning lowlands into huge lakes for a few days.

▲The true course of this Indian river is hard to see, for both sides have overflowed, and drowned huge stretches of farmland. Floods happen here in most years after heavy rain.

STRANGE SIGHTS

▲This photograph shows a pale, thin, shimmering layer like far-off water on the ground. This is a mirage and is really the sky reflected by a layer of hot air. Such mirages often happen in hot weather.

Unusual weather conditions can play tricks with our eyes. Sometimes we see coloured lights in the sky or even objects that are not really there.

Rainbows

When you see a rainbow arching through the sky its many-coloured bands seem to have both ends on the ground. Yet as you move towards it, the rainbow keeps retreating, and most rainbows fade quickly.

If you look carefully you will see that the rainbow is made up of seven bands, each a different colour. From top to bottom these colours are red, orange, yellow, green, blue, indigo and violet. Above this bright *primary rainbow* you can often see a fainter 'secondary' bow. This bow's colours are reversed, with violet on top and red below. Very occasionally you can even see a third bow.

Rainbows only show up when the sun is low behind you and shining on a shower of rain or spray. This holds a clue to why rainbows appear. In fact they are simply sunlight bent and reflected by drops of water in air. Sunlight passing through a raindrop is bounced back from its far side which acts like a mirror. But sunlight bends as it passes from air to water or water to air. This bending separates the seven colours that make up white sunlight. Each colour reaches your eyes from a slightly different direction and this is why the different colours show as separate bands.

A main or primary rainbow appears when droplets reflect light only once. A secondary rainbow comes from droplets that reflect light twice. Extra reflections produce even more rainbows, but the more times a raindrop reflects light, the weaker the rainbows grow.

Mirages

Mirage comes from a Latin word meaning 'to look at'. Mirages are strange effects of light produced by different air layers. Just as light bends as it passes from air to water or back, so light bends as it passes between a cool, dense air layer and a layer that is warmer and less dense. This bending makes objects appear to be where they are not.

On a hot summer day you might seem to see a pool of water lying in the distance on the road ahead. In fact what you are really seeing is the sky. Light rays that slant down from the sky bend upward as they reach a layer of hot air above the road, but below eye level. So the rays reach your eye as if rising from the ground. This also happens in a desert. Thirsty travellers often think they see a lake far off among the barren rock and sand.

Mirages which appear below the object that they show are called *inferior mirages*. Mirages appearing above the object that they show are superior mirages. Superior mirages occur when cold, dense air forms a layer with its upper surface just above your eye level. Light rays from distant mountains bend

▼A different type of 'rainbow' photographed near the English coast on a stormy day. In the distance are towering cumulonimbus clouds.

downward as they reach the cold dense air. So the rays reach your eye as if slanting down from somewhere high above the real mountains. Their peaks seem floating in the sky. Superior mirages can even show mountain ranges that really lie out of sight below the horizon.

WEATHER FORECASTING

▲A radiosonde rises from a weather station in a harsh polar land. The balloon lifts instruments high in the atmosphere to measure weather up there. A radio sends signals to earth where the weathermen study them.

SENIOR FORECASTER

▲Meteorologists at work preparing the next day's forecast. In front of them is a map of the fronts and pressure regions over the north Atlantic and northern Europe.

If you plan a picnic you need to know if the day will be wet or dry, warm or cold. Farmers need to know when the weather will be good for sowing, spraying, or harvesting. Seamen and airline pilots need warnings of fogs or fierce winds. So weather forecasts have many uses.

There is an old saying, 'Red sky at night, shepherd's delight; red sky in the morning, shepherd's warning'. To some extent this is true: most of our weather approaches from the west, so that a red sunset, which only occurs when skies to the west are clear, implies fine weather. Red morning skies, showing clear skies to the east, tell us little. Most attempts to forecast weather from a little information from one place are useless. Professional meteorologists use weather observations made at the same time from hundreds of weather stations. They also get valuable information from ships, aircraft, satellites and from instruments carried up by balloons.

Instruments that measure weather

Weather stations have special instruments to measure air pressure, wind speed and direction, humidity, temperature and rainfall. The observer also notes cloud types and amounts, as well as visibility, and sends all the information once an hour to a collecting centre. From there the data is transmitted all over the world.

Atmospheric pressure is measured by an instrument called a *barometer* or, if it draws a line showing the rise and fall of pressure on a sheet of paper, it is called a *barograph*. The simplest barometer balances atmospheric pressure, which is the weight of air, against a column of mercury. Falling pressure hints that a depression or storm is on the way. Rising pressure suggests an anticyclone may be bringing settled weather.

Wind speed and direction are measured by an *anemometer*. This instrument must not be too near the ground or shielded by buildings or trees. The speed is measured by the rate of rotation of cups on a rotor arm. Direction is shown by a special type of weather vane which lines up with the wind. These mechanisms convert speed and direction into electric currents which produce readings on a dial. An easy way of judging wind speed was devised in the early 1800s by the British admiral Sir Francis Beaufort. He intended it for ships at sea, but it has now been altered a little and is used on land as well. The Beaufort Scale divides wind strength into 12 forces. Calm air is force 0. A gentle breeze that rustles leaves is force 3. A gale that snaps twigs off trees and makes walking difficult is force 8. A hurricane that uproots trees and rips the roofs off houses is force 12.

Temperature is measured by an ordinary mercury in glass thermometer. The mercury in this expands, rising as temperatures rise. But it is no good putting the thermometer just anywhere. Meteorologists all put thermometers in the same kind of container – a *Stevenson screen*. This is a box on legs standing 1.2 m (4 ft) above the ground. Air flows through the louvred sides and around the instruments, but they are shielded from the rain and sun.

Humidity – the amount of moisture in the air – is worked out from readings from a second thermometer in the Stevenson screen. This has wet muslin wrapped around the bulb. Evaporating moisture takes heat from the wet bulb so this wet-bulb thermometer shows a lower temperature than the dry-bulb thermometer. The *relative humidity* of air depends on the difference between their temperatures. Both temperatures and humidity can also be recorded as a line drawn on paper wrapped round a slowly rotating drum. A *thermograph* measures temperature and a *hygrograph* measures humidity. The thermograph uses a coil made of different metals which winds or unwinds as temperatures fall or rise. The hygrograph uses a hair which absorbs moisture and expands in humid conditions and shortens when it becomes drier.

Making a weather forecast

Meteorologists at weather stations all around the world make observations at set times and convert them into codes which can be understood by their colleagues everywhere, whatever their nationality. At the larger centres these observations, together with others from aircraft, satellites and balloons, are carefully checked and fed into computers.

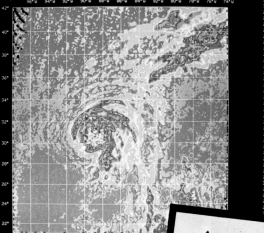

◀This was hurricane Camille as seen from a weather satellite high above. Different colours show areas with different temperatures. High, cool clouds appear blue, grey or yellow. Sea, cloud and land are warmer. The warmest regions of all appear purple.

▶Anemometers have a spinning propeller or spinning cups that measure wind speed. The greater this speed the faster they spin. A vane shows wind direction.

Weather charts are drawn, sometimes by computer, to show the positions of depressions and anticyclones, together with zones of strong winds, and the boundaries of warm or cold air masses known as fronts.

Short-range weather forecasts of just a few hours may be made from radar pictures showing areas of rain within the nearest 320 km (200 miles) or so, together with recent charts. Beyond this it is necessary to forecast the movement of weather systems. In recent years meteorologists have used the most powerful computers in the world to imitate the atmosphere as huge quantities of numbers, but it takes many millions of calculations even for one day's forecast!

Special forecasts are produced for aircraft, shipping, farmers and anybody else who has a particular need for one.

ALTERING THE WEATHER

Rain, rain, go away.
Come again another day.

Maybe you have said that rhyme when rain spoilt a day out in the countryside or by the sea. Preventing rain may be just wishful thinking. Yet people can and do deliberately try to alter the weather in some ways.

Altering weather at will
Farmers can help to protect their fields and orchards from frosts and gales that damage crops. In spring, if frost seems likely, some fruit farmers spray water droplets in the air. These form a fog that hangs above the trees and stops heat escaping into space. Thus no frost forms to injure tender fruit blossoms.

Farmers sometimes grow tall hedges around vineyards and hopfields, and lines of trees around fields where the land is very flat. The hedges slow down the wind, so preventing gales damaging the grapes and hops. They also stop the topsoil blowing away when the ground is dry.

People even try bringing rain to thirsty crops by tampering with clouds. The idea is to sprinkle clouds with special crystals in the hope that water vapour will condense on the crystals to build ice particles or water droplets. These might then produce drops of rain. In South Dakota farmers pay for planes to drop silver iodide crystals on the clouds. But not all weather experts are sure that this produces any extra rain.

Summer hailstorms can sometimes flatten crops. In Yugoslavia, where this is quite a problem, special rockets are fired into the storm clouds. The Russians use special anti-aircraft shells instead. The idea is to make the clouds produce tiny particles of ice instead of the large hailstones that do the damage.

Foggy airport runways can make it difficult for planes to land. At Orly Airport, Paris, engineers set up 15 powerful jet engines to try to blast the fog away. But no airports have yet found a cheap, effective way of clearing foggy air.

Altering weather by accident
Most man-made weather changes are very small. But much larger changes can come about by accident.

Take city weather, for example. Just by being there a city can affect its weather. On hot, humid days, city streets and buildings give off more heat than the green countryside around. Sometimes, in showery conditions, hot, moist air rises high above the city. By afternoon, a storm cloud may have grown and produced a heavy shower. Meanwhile, much of the countryside around might stay quite dry and sunny.

In winter, the heat from city buildings can be enough to warm city air and prevent frosts or fog forming. Winter is always warmer in big cities like London, New York, Rome or Paris, than on the farms nearby.

Not only cities warm air. Around the world heat escapes from the engines of millions of trucks, cars, trains, planes and ships, and from the fires that people burn. Burning fuels produce huge quantities of waste carbon dioxide gas. This gas is a natural part of air, but it is a slowly increasing part. Many scientists believe it is warming the world's weather. This is because the sun's rays can penetrate the

▼This diagram shows two likely effects of dropping silver iodide crystals on clouds. Cloud droplets freeze around the crystals to form artificial ice particles. These may fall and melt to give rain. Or warm, rising air might make them melt and evaporate. If that happens the ground below stays dry.

artificial ice particle
layers of ice
silver iodide crystal

silver iodide bomb

silver iodide bomb

artificial ice particles

ice evaporated by warm air before reaching earth

ice melts to form rain

rising warm air.

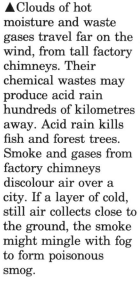

carbon dioxide to warm the earth, but carbon dioxide absorbs some of the heat radiated by the earth, so that it cannot escape into space. In other words, the carbon dioxide acts in the same way as a greenhouse roof. The world seems to have warmed up slightly in the last few years. If warming up continues, over many hundreds of years, the world might one day grow so hot that all the ice melts. Then the sea would rise, drowning many cities and huge areas of land all over the earth.

Meanwhile man tampers with the air in other ways. Some burning fuels give off smoke and poisonous gases. Cities, factories and vehicles pour out huge amounts of substances that poison, or pollute, the air. Strong winds or rising air usually clear away the smoke and gases. Eventually the larger particles fall to earth and rain brings down most of the others. But on some winter days a layer of cold, still air lies just above the ground. This air traps smoke and gases and they may mix with fog to make the dirty yellow mixture known as smog. Smog injures people's lungs and slowly gnaws into the stone of certain buildings.

The damage caused by smog is now recognized in many countries, which have laws to make smokeless zones. As a result smog is rare.

Forest fires sometimes affect huge tracts of countryside. Volcanoes can give out huge amounts of smoke and ash which some meteorologists believe can lead to changes in the weather over considerable areas.

Man interferes with the upper air as well. High-flying planes leave vapour trails made up of tiny ice crystals. Some experts fear that the increasing use of aerosol sprays with certain propellant gases could lead to chemical reactions in the upper atmosphere, which would lead to more harmful radiation reaching the earth.

▲Clouds of hot moisture and waste gases travel far on the wind, from tall factory chimneys. Their chemical wastes may produce acid rain hundreds of kilometres away. Acid rain kills fish and forest trees. Smoke and gases from factory chimneys discolour air over a city. If a layer of cold, still air collects close to the ground, the smoke might mingle with fog to form poisonous smog.

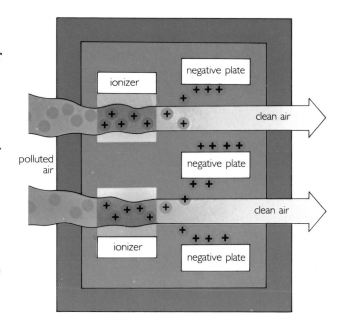

◀An electrostatic precipitator helps some factories to clean air from their chimneys. Blue arrows show polluted air sucked into the precipitator. An ionizer gives particles in the air a positive electrical charge (shown as a plus sign). Negatively charged plates attract these particles, so they stick to the plates. This leaves the air cleaner than before.

2 WEATHER AROUND THE WORLD

climatic regions

	tropical forest	continually hot ; heavy rainfall throughout year
	savanna	hot summers, warm winters ; wet in summer
	tropical steppe	continually hot ; little rainfall
	continental steppe	warm summers, cold winters ; little precipitation
	tropical desert	continually hot ; little rainfall
	continental desert	hot summers, cold winters ; little precipitation
	subtropical	hot summers, mild winters ; moderate precipitation
	temperate	warm summers, cool winters ; moderate precipitation
	subarctic	short cool summers, long cold winters ; little precipitation
	tundra	short cold summers, long very cold winters ; little precipitation
	highland	cooler than surrounding areas
	icecap	continually cold ; little precipitation

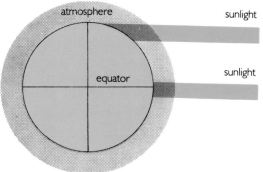

INTRODUCTION

Weather varies hugely from place to place around the world. The simplest way to compare weather is by looking at different climates. The climate of a continent, a country, or a town is its usual weather measured over many years. Some climates are warm, others cold, some wet, some dry. Certain climates have mild, rainy winters and hot dry summers; other climates are hot and rainy all year round. Geographers divide the world into a number of climatic regions.

The ingredients of climate

Each region's climate depends on several ingredients. The main one is latitude – distance north or south of the equator. Near the equator the sun shines down hotly every day from almost directly overhead. Near the poles the sun does not even rise at all for months, and much of the year is bitterly cold.

Another important ingredient of climate is altitude, or height above sea level. The higher you climb, the colder the air becomes. This is true at the equator as well as in polar regions. Everywhere high mountain tops are much colder than the valleys below them.

Land and sea affect climate, too. Land warms up faster than water in summer, but cools down faster in winter. So cities in the middle of a continent will have hotter summers and colder winters than cities on the coast. Then, too, winds pick up moisture as they cross a sea, so they may shed rain on the coast. But by the time the winds have blown far inland they may be quite dry. So coasts, especially if they face west, generally have more rain than places far inland.

Inside each climatic region are places with special, local climates. Large lakes are cooler in summer and warmer in winter than the countryside around. Hillsides might be warm or cool according to whether they face towards or away from the sun. Some slopes are more open to cold winds than others. Valley hollows suffer more frosts than valley slopes. And so on.

Climate and living things

A climate has a great effect upon the people living in it. A hot damp climate makes people feel lazy. A cool climate makes them feel energetic. Some climates are so cold that people always need to dress up warmly. Other climates are so hot that people can wear light clothing all the year.

Climate affects soil and plants, too. Soil is made of crumbled rock and the nourishing remains of plant and animal matter. But rainy climates wash plant foods deep down, while dry climates leave them near the surface. So different climates help produce different kinds of soil.

Plants are clues to the climate of an area. Only low-growing hardy plants survive in the world's coldest places. Hardy evergreen trees grow where summers are warm or cool, and winters long and cold. You find deciduous trees, trees that shed their leaves in winter, where winters are fairly short and not very cold. Tall, evergreen broadleaved trees flourish in warm, moist climates. Grass covers much of the drier land in warm and cool climates. Only drought-defying plants, such as cacti, survive in the driest climates.

Crops as well as wild plants vary with the local climate. For instance, rice likes warm, rainy conditions; corn prefers less rain, and warm or hot summers but cool or cold winters.

The animals that live in different regions depend upon both the climate and the vegetation. This chapter looks at different climates, one by one, and how these affect life around the world.

◄This map shows one way of dividing the world into climatic regions. The small diagram helps to show why climate is hotter at the equator than at the poles. To reach the north pole sunlight must pass through more air than sunlight that shines on the equator. So the northern sunlight loses more heat to the atmosphere and is also spread out more thinly.

SEASONS

In most climates the year is divided into different seasons. In spring, the sun climbs a little higher in the sky each day; daylight lasts a little longer, and the weather grows warmer. In summer, the sun shines down at mid-day from the highest point it reaches all the year. Summer has the longest days and warmest weather. In autumn the sun sinks a little lower every day and nights lengthen. In winter the sun is at its lowest for the year. Winter is the season of the shortest days and coldest weather.

What causes seasons

Seasons happen because of how the earth journeys around the sun.

The earth is always spinning on its axis, an imaginary line between the north and south poles. Each spin, or rotation, takes 24 hours – the length of a day and a night. As the earth spins, its sun-facing side has daylight and the side in shadow has night. It takes 365¼ days (or spins) for the earth to travel once around the sun. That time is the length of one earth year.

The earth spins at an angle, like a spinning top always tilted in the same direction. A lamp and an orange will show you how this helps produce the seasons. The lamp stands for the sun. The orange represents the earth. Hold the orange level with the lamp, in a dark room. Tilt the orange so that your lamp (the 'sun') shines on the stem-end (the

'north pole') of the orange. Now rotate the orange on its axis, to imitate the spinning earth. Your north pole stays lit up all the time, but your south pole stays dark. That happens day after day when it is summer in the northern hemisphere, the northern half of the world. In summer, day lasts longer than night everywhere north of the equator. The farther north you go, the longer daylight lasts. The very longest day is called the summer solstice. On this day, 21 or 22 June, the sun at mid-day is directly over the tropic of Cancer at 23½° north of the equator.

Keep the axis of your orange pointing in the same direction and move it one quarter of the way around your lamp. Rotate the orange as before. Notice that light now reaches all parts of the rotating orange. This happens to the earth one day in spring and one in autumn, when the noonday sun shines down directly above the equator. On these days, 21 March and 23 September, day lasts as long as night everywhere on earth. These days are called equinoxes, a word meaning 'equal nights'. The northern hemisphere of your orange now has its autumn equinox.

Keep the axis of your orange pointing in the same direction as before and move the orange another quarter of the way around your lamp. Since your orange started moving it has travelled half way around the lamp. Rotate the orange as before. Now the lamp (the 'sun') shines on the south pole of the orange all the time but the north pole lies in darkness. That happens day after day when it is winter in the northern hemisphere. When the north pole's tilt takes it farthest from the sun, the northern hemisphere has the year's longest night and shortest day. That day is the winter solstice. It occurs on 22 or 23 December when the sun at mid-day is directly over the tropic of Capricorn at 23½° south.

Now move your orange another quarter of the way around the lamp. This brings the orange to another equinox. On earth this is the spring equinox in the northern hemisphere and the autumn equinox in the southern hemisphere.

▼Four diagrams show sunlight falling on the earth at different seasons. In summer, the north pole (N) leans towards the sun, so day lasts longer than night at place **a** in the northern hemisphere. In autumn and spring, place **a** has days and nights of almost equal length. In winter, **a**'s nights are longer than days. The diagram seems to show the earth's tilt changing with the seasons. In fact the earth always tilts in the same direction, but its path around the sun means each hemisphere leans towards the sun for only half the year.

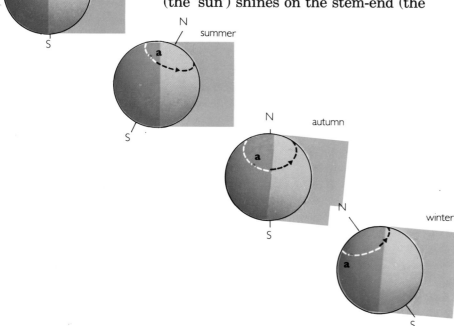

▲A woodland glade in spring with fresh grass appearing and the first of the young leaves sprouting. Plenty of light reaches the ground and flowers such as primroses and violets will grow.

▲By midsummer the trees are thickly covered with leaves and little sunlight reaches the ground. There will be few flowers and not very much grass.

▲Autumn woods take on a golden glow as dying leaves turn from green to red, brown and yellow. Then they drop to carpet the ground.

►By winter some shrubs and trees have lost all their leaves. The air is cold enough for frost to form and snow to fall.

TROPICAL RAINY CLIMATES

In most countries one season is much warmer or wetter than another. But close to the equator there are no seasons. Here, people have much the same kind of weather day after day all through the year.

You find this equatorial type of climate in the tropical rain forests of Central and South America, west and west-central Africa, Malaysia, Indonesia and much of southern Vietnam.

Here, nights last about as long as days and there is very little twilight. The noonday sun shines from almost overhead, so every day is hot. By early afternoon the temperature is over 27°C (81°F). Temperatures stay high even at night. At sea level only about 2°C (3.6°F) separate the year's highest and lowest noonday temperature in most places.

Besides being very hot, the air is always humid. This means that perspiration cannot evaporate, but trickles uncomfortably down your skin. Then, too, the air is almost always still. There are no cooling breezes, except near coasts. Just walking around is quite an effort in the hot, sticky heat.

Rain every day

Near the equator weather is similar from day to day, but it alters hour by hour. Most mornings start with clear blue skies. But by early afternoon the sun's heat has drawn a huge amount of water vapour into the atmosphere. As the warm, moist air rises it cools and clouds form. By mid-afternoon, fluffy cumulus clouds have built up into towering cumulonimbus. Rain falls in torrents from them and there are often thunderstorms. By evening, as the sun sets, the clouds break up and fade away.

Most equatorial places receive plenty of rain, spread evenly all through the year. Some oceanic islands have tremendous rainfall. The Pacific Island of Jaluit gets about 450 cm (177 in) of rain each year.

Life in a rain forest

Plants and creatures that need a warm, moist climate thrive close to the equator.

Here, plants grow fast and close together. One scientist worked out that there must be 64 million plants in each square mile (2.6 sq km) in the forests of southern Malaya. Here, too, plants grow in great variety. A Dutch botanist reckoned that Indonesia must have 30,000 species of flowering plant. That is 15 times as many kinds as in the British Isles. There are so many species of

▼Palms are among the trees that flourish in the world's hot, steamy forests. But there you seldom see so many trees of one kind close together. These coconut palms in Sri Lanka may have been planted for their fruit.

tropical rain-forest plant that thousands have yet to be described.

A tropical forest's plants form several layers. The highest layer is a sea of touching tree tops high above the ground. Tall, straight trunks like mighty pillars hold their leafy crowns up to the light. Below this canopy come smaller trees, tree ferns and lianas. Lianas are woody climbers that can grow as thick as a man's thigh and more than 100 m (328 ft) long. In the dim light lower down, ferns and other soft-stemmed plants rise from the forest floor. The floor itself has a covering of rotted leaves and wood, and sprouting fungi.

Warmth-loving creatures live at every level in the forest. Most kinds live off the ground. Gaudy butterflies, monkeys, and such birds as parrots feed among the flowers and fruits of the tree tops. High up, tree frogs breed in rainwater puddles filling leafy cups. Tree snakes slither in search of prey. The forest floor is home to many mammals: rodents, hogs, antelopes, jaguars and tigers.

People are chopping down huge areas of tropical forest for timber, or burning it to clear the land for farming. Soon, very little could remain outside the heart of South America and Africa.

►Moisture-loving ferns grow close together where light filters down between forest trees. In tropical rain forests undergrowth thrives best on stream banks and in clearings where old forest has been burnt down or felled.

◄This bird's eye view shows the touching tree tops of the Amazonian forest, the world's largest tropical rain forest. It covers much of the huge region of South America called Amazonia. The bare strip is part of the Trans-Amazonian Highway, one of the world's longest forest roads.

►Broad-leaved banana plants and low shrubs crowd together as they thrust up into the light at the forest rim. Beyond, grow the tall broad-leaved, hardwood trees that thrive in a tropical rain forest.

MONSOON CLIMATES

If you live in North America or Europe, you probably expect each year to have four seasons. There may be a cold winter, a cool spring, a warm summer and a mild autumn. Changes from one season to another are gradual and any season may be wet or dry. Large parts of the world, however, are quite different. In most of the tropics it is always warm or hot and there are only two main seasons: one is wet, the other dry. Such places have a monsoon type of climate.

The word monsoon means a seasonal wind and comes from *mausim*, the Arabic word for 'season'. Monsoon climates depend on winds that blow from opposite directions in different seasons. Winds bring torrential rain from nearby oceans in summer, but dry winds blow off the land in winter.

A summer monsoon works like this. In summer, land in the tropics becomes much hotter than the sea. The land heats the air above it, which becomes less dense and this creates a large low-pressure area over the land. Meanwhile air above the sea stays cooler and denser with relatively high pressure. Low-level winds blow from the sea towards the land to replace air that has been rising. These winds hold a great deal of water vapour that has evaporated from the sea, and as they reach land they produce heavy rain.

Some of the world's heaviest rain falls where moist sea air cools as it rises to cross mountain ranges.

A winter monsoon works in the opposite way. In winter, the land is colder than the sea. So a dense mass of cool or cold air covers the land. Now air pressure is higher over land than over sea, so winds blow from the land towards the sea. Because not much moisture evaporates from the land, winds blowing off the land are dry and in a winter monsoon no rain may fall for months.

The best-known monsoon lands lie just north and south of the rainy tropics which form a broad belt with the equator running through the middle.

The most extensive monsoon region lies around the southern and eastern rim of Asia, the largest continent. In summer, south-westerly winds from the Indian and Pacific oceans blow into Asia and bring rain to India, Burma, Indonesia and China. In winter, north-easterly winds blow out from deep inside Asia and keep much of these countries completely dry for months. Some coastal parts of southern North America and northern South America also have monsoon-type rains. So do coastal regions of West and East Africa and northern Australia.

In the northern hemisphere, the rainy season sets in at the end of May. Rain

►On this map yellow areas show the world's main monsoon regions. Most lie in broad belts on either side of the equator. Red arrows show where winds bring summer rain as they blow in off the sea.

pours in torrents for days at a time throughout June, July and August. At last the winds slacken and the rain grows lighter. By late October it may have stopped. Indeed, three-quarters of the year's rainfall often arrives in just three months.

In the southern hemisphere, January and February are northern Australia's wettest months.

Not all monsoon regions are alike. In parts of South-East Asia and Australia some rain falls in every month, although one season is particularly wet. Outside the warm tropics lie some much cooler monsoon regions, such as the eastern Soviet Union where winter temperatures drop far below freezing.

Even in a single monsoon region, wet and dry seasons are not always exactly the same from year to year. In India, for instance, some summers are wetter than others. Now and then the rain is very late or very little. Sometimes years pass without any rain at all.

Life in a monsoon climate

The wild plants and animals in many monsoon lands are able to survive months of drought. The great teak trees of India and South-East Asia are one example. When dry weather starts teak trees shed all their leaves. This almost completely stops moisture escaping from the trees. If they kept their leaves the trees would just dry up and die. In even drier lands you find tall grasses and small trees. Grass dies in the drought, but when rain arrives, new shoots soon sprout from roots or seeds. Elephants, monkeys, lions and tigers are among the animals found in one or another of the monsoon regions of the tropics.

Farmers living in monsoon regions have learnt to grow crops that make the most of summer rain. People grow food plants such as beans, peanuts, rice and sugar cane. Tea and cotton are important, too. And avocado, banana and mango fruits grow here. But when rains fail crops wither and food gets scarce. In such years many people go hungry, and some starve.

▲Monsoon rains fill terraced rice fields on a steep slope in Nepal. Here, in the Himalayas, the rice crop depends on these rains, because outside the rainy season the ground is too dry for such crops to grow.

▶Umbrellas shelter Indians from a heavy downpour. They have gathered to celebrate the start of the monsoon rains. These cool the air, which had been unbearably hot. They also bring much-needed moisture that helps crops grow.

THE GREAT GRASSLANDS

►Rough grass and scattered, bushy trees spread far across Kenya's Tsavo National Park. The dry dusty ground shows that this is savanna in the dry season.

▼Bison still graze among the grasses, herbs and shrubs of this North American prairie. But most of this great wild grassland is now grazed by cattle or ploughed up and sown with crops.

Looking out over a great stretch of grassland is rather like gazing out to sea. The land stretches flat and open to the horizon. The wind sends waves through the grasses, much as waves travel through the surface of the sea. Natural grasslands of this kind receive no rain for months each year. Then come summer showers. But not all natural grassland is the same. Tropical grasslands are warmer than temperate grasslands farther from the equator, and they have different kinds of grasses.

Tropical grassland

Tropical grassland, or savanna, covers much of Africa and parts of South America, and India. Many of these places have a monsoon climate (see page 40).

Savanna lies on either side of the equator; much savanna is sandwiched between the tropical rain forests of the equatorial region and the world's hot deserts. Tropical grasslands tend to have dry, warm winters and wet, warm summers. The dryness comes from the mass of warm, dry air that lies above some continents, or from dry Trade Winds that have blown overland, so bring little moisture. After months of dry air and cloudless skies, the weather grows extremely hot. Soon afterwards, the summer rains begin. This happens as moist, hot air moves out from the equator, bringing heavy showers.

The main savanna plants are tall grasses. African elephant grass grows much higher than a man. In winter, grass blades turn brown and die. But when the rains begin, green shoots soon push up above ground and take their place. Scrawny thorn trees and fat-trunked baobab trees sprout here and there in damper hollows. So some savanna looks like an open park with scattered trees.

Wild animals of many kinds find food and shelter in savanna lands. Large herds of antelopes and zebras roam the upland plains of Africa. Lions, leopards, hyaenas and packs of fierce wild hunting dogs run down and kill any large plant-

eating beasts too slow to run away.

But herdsmen and farmers have begun taking over the savanna for their cattle and such crops as maize. Sometimes they burn huge areas of grass to encourage the new shoots their herds enjoy eating.

Temperate grasslands
The largest temperate grasslands are the prairies in the heart of North America and the steppes which stretch from eastern Europe into Central Asia. Other temperate grasslands cover parts of south-east South America, Central Asia, southern Africa, south-east Australia and south-east New Zealand. On steppes and prairies, rain falls mostly in the warm summer months. Deep in North America and Asia, winter is usually dry and very cold.

The grasses in these lands are shorter than savanna grasses and they are often mixed with brightly flowering soft-stemmed plants like poppies. But farmers and herdsmen have moved in, and huge tracts of steppe and prairie have been ploughed up or used for grazing sheep and cattle.

Geographers once thought the world's great grasslands stood on land too dry for forest trees. But experts have found that many trees could grow on some parts of Africa's savanna if farm animals and

◀Cacti and bunches of tough grasses are among the scattered plants growing on the cold, dry *puna*. This is steppe-like countryside high among the Andes mountains of Bolivia in South America.

people left the land alone. Many people now think that much savanna land was forest long ago. They believe, too, that trees might have been quite plentiful in steppe and prairie countryside. Trees could grow again if people stopped digging up and burning grassland and letting sheep, cattle and especially goats nibble all the plants that try to sprout.

▼Long, green grass sprouts as high as a giraffe's knees in an East African savanna. This is the rainy season, when moisture soaks the soil and plants put out new growth. Clouds building overhead might mean more rain is on the way.

DESERTS

If you drop a piece of paper on the ground, rain will probably soon soak it and it will gradually rot away. But this does not happen in deserts, the driest lands on earth. In some deserts no rain falls for years, so nothing rots. Bodies buried in desert sands dry up but their skin survives for centuries.

Great belts of desert lie on the edges of the tropics. Some deserts stay dry because they lie deep inland, far from the winds bringing moisture from the sea. Most deserts lie below the gently sinking, drying air of the sub-tropical high pressure area (page 20). Other deserts lie under winds that have shed their moisture as they rose to cross mountains. Yet other deserts occur where moist sea winds reach heated land after blowing across a cold sea current. Many deserts stay dry for a mixture of such reasons.

Deserts around the world

If you include Antarctica and parts of Spain, every continent has at least one desert. A great belt of hot desert stretches from north-west Africa to India. North Africa's Sahara is the largest desert in the world. It covers almost as much land as the United States. Hot deserts also sprawl over south-west North America. In the southern hemisphere, hot desert fills the centre of Australia and much of western South America and south-west Africa.

The world's cooler deserts lie farther from the equator – in places like eastern Central Asia, and Patagonia, the dry south-east of South America.

Deserts are not all as dry as one

▼Wind ripples the sandy surface here in the Sahara Desert. No plants can root in such shifting sands. But most of the Sahara has a stonier surface where at least some desert plants grow.

▼Like most oases, this one in Morocco is intensively cultivated and highly productive. The small area of green is a marked contrast to the surrounding desert.

another. Patagonia has 13–15 cm (5–6 in) of rain each year. But part of the Atacama Desert in Chile appears to have had no rain for 400 years until 1972 when rain poured down in torrents. Many deserts get what rain they have like that, in sudden bursts that come at unexpected times.

Desert temperatures also vary. Hot deserts can be very hot indeed. Part of the Sahara once reached 58°C (136.4°F). This is probably the world's highest-ever measured shade temperature. Yet even the Sahara can be cold at night in winter. Because there are no clouds to trap heat near the ground, warmth quickly radiates into space. Night frosts can occur.

Winds often blow across deserts. Small whirlwinds called dust devils pick up dust and writhe across the desert floor like twisting pillars. There are also dust storms – large, whirling masses of dust-filled air. Sandstorms are desert winds strong enough to lift sand grains high above the ground. The Simoom is a scorching-hot kind of sandstorm that sometimes roars across the Sahara.

Life in desert climates

Life is difficult for plants and animals in deserts, and even more difficult for humans. Drying up is the biggest danger. But things that live in deserts have ways to beat the drought. Desert plants like cacti survive by storing water in fat stems with waterproof outer skins. Other plants spring up from seeds just after rain. These plants soon die. But their seeds survive for months or even years, waiting for the next heavy rain before they start to sprout.

Desert mice and lizards can lick dew from plants and stones. Camels lose no moisture as sweat until their bodies grow extremely hot; even then their bodies can lose a great deal of water before they need to drink.

Some deserts get almost hot enough by day to cook the animals that live there. Lizards, mice and snakes escape the noonday heat by burrowing. Also, sidewinding desert snakes slither sideways in a way that always keeps part of the body off the scorching sand.

Desert peoples mostly roam the desert edges with their flocks and herds, continually searching for new vegetation. These wanderers are called nomads.

▶Big cacti jut from the floor of Mexico's Sonora Desert. When rare rains fall they quickly take up moisture. Their fat stems can store water for months.

◀Sub-tropical deserts, although not as extreme in climate as the tropical deserts, are still exceedingly hostile environments for plants and animals. Long roots help plants tap water far below the dry surface soil.

TEMPERATE CLIMATES

Between the sub-tropical deserts and the cold polar regions lie lands with temperate climates. Here, the weather is neither always hot nor always cold. This description fits much of North America and Europe, and parts of southern South America, southern Africa, southern Australia and New Zealand.

These places owe their temperate climates to a complicated clash between warm subtropical air moving towards the poles and colder air pushing outward from the polar regions. Where these air masses meet, depressions form and travel eastwards, bringing strong winds and snow or rain. But anticyclones sometimes form and block the paths of depressions. These areas of high pressure bring warm, still, sunny summer weather or chilly days and frosty nights in winter. So the weather in much of Europe and North America is very changeable.

Exactly where and when depressions and anticyclones form depends on what happens high above the earth. Fast-moving rivers of air about 10 km (6 miles) high are always speeding from west to east around the northern and southern hemispheres. A balloon set free in such a river or jet stream would take only two weeks to drift round the world. But it would not travel by the shortest route. The jet stream takes a zigzag path. In the northern hemisphere each northward 'zig' carries warm air towards the north pole. Each southward 'zag' takes cold air south towards the equator. Each zig and each zag affects the weather on the ground or sea below. Sometimes the jet stream spreads out, encouraging air beneath to rise and helping a stormy depression form. In other parts the stream may narrow, helping to build pressure beneath with descending air creating the fine weather of an anticyclone.

The whole jet stream moves north and weakens during summer. As a result the depressions tend to form further north and are usually weaker.

Cool temperate climates

Temperate climates with a cold season are called 'cool temperate'. Such places include British Columbia, Oregon and Washington in North America, and the British Isles, southern Scandinavia and

►Deciduous woods and mixed forests were the original vegetation of most of the temperate climatic regions of the world. Almost everywhere these have been cleared to make way for agriculture.

Oaks are typical of the trees that grow in the world's cool temperate regions. They need plenty of rain and shed their leaves in winter to avoid the damaging effects of frost and snow.

This spring scene is set in the Mediterranean island of Crete. The spring flowers will soon wither when the hot, dry summer starts. But the tough-leaved olive trees stay green all the year.

western Europe.

In all these places, where the prevailing westerly winds cross large oceans, the weather often changes. Depressions bringing rain or drizzle are followed by sunny intervals and showers, and intervals of fine anticyclonic weather. In winter, inland areas and mountains get snow and frost, although it is rarer on coasts. Summers are mostly warm and not often very hot.

In the southern hemisphere, southern Chile, Tasmania and New Zealand's South Island also have this climate.

Cool temperate climates suit deciduous trees like oaks which shed their leaves in winter. Here, too, live animals such as skunks, squirrels and hedgehogs that hibernate – spend the winter asleep.

Cool temperate regions have some of the world's best land for raising cattle, sheep and crops like cereals, apples and potatoes.

Warm temperate climates

A warm temperate climate is one with hot summers and mild winters. Places like this lie nearer the equator than places with a cool temperate climate. Those with oceans to the west have long, hot, dry summers because travelling depressions have moved further north or south. The winters are mild and rainy. You find this climate in central California, central Chile, in parts of south-west South Africa and south-west Australia, and around the Mediterranean Sea. In fact this climate has been called the Mediterranean climate.

Lands with oceans to the east also have hot summers and mild winters, but their rain is spread throughout the year. This is what you find in the south-east United States, around the River Plate in South America, in south-east South Africa, south-east Australia and New Zealand's North Island.

Tough-leaved shrubs and trees, like the olive and the carob, and animals like tortoises and lizards survive the summer droughts easily.

Warm temperate climates are where farmers grow most of the world's grapes and citrus crops like oranges and lemons.

47

▲Conifers like these form the great forests that stretch across northern continents. Conifers are rich in sticky resin. This oozes out to seal off damaged wood and so helps to prevent rotting.

COLD FOREST CLIMATES

Suppose a spacecraft took you whizzing above North America, Europe and Asia where these continents are broadest. You would gaze down upon a mighty belt of trees. This is the boreal, or northern, forest, which forms an immense band around the northern hemisphere. In fact it is the largest belt of forest anywhere.

This vast region has a harsh kind of climate all its own. In winter, a huge, cold, dry area of high pressure is overhead. Winter is long and very cold, with snow. In summer, air pressure drops. The summer can be warm or even hot, but with some showery or stormy spells. Most rain falls at this time of the year. But summer is soon over, especially in the far north or south.

There are two reasons for this climate. First, most northern forest lies too far from the equator to be always warm. Secondly, most lies far inland, so it is really out of reach of sea winds bringing mild, moist air. As a result, these inland regions have colder winters but warmer summers than the coasts. Also these inland places have little winter snow and not much summer rain.

Shivering and sweltering

The switch from winter cold to summer heat is almost unbelievable in some inland towns. At Verkhoyansk in the north-east Soviet Union, winter temperatures can plunge to −70°C (−94°F). Yet the summer temperature once reached 36.7°C (98°F). This gives Verkhoyansk the world record for range in temperatures.

Life in northern forests

Only cold-proof trees survive in northern forests. Most are firs, pines, or other conifers – trees bearing seeds on cones. The needle-shaped leaves have thick skins that stop moisture escaping. This prevents drying out in dry or frosty weather. Many conifers are shaped like pyramids to help snow slip off them, instead of breaking their branches. Yet winters are so cold that the sap may freeze in some trees, and their trunks split with a bang.

Northern forests are the home of the moose or elk, the world's largest deer. Immense brown bears and that wild cat, the northern lynx, also roam among the conifers.

Short summers make farming difficult, so most people living here are foresters or miners. But some farm or trap forest animals, like mink and foxes, for their fur.

►The magnificent General Sherman tree growing among smaller giant sequoias in the Sierra Nevada mountains of California. Unlike most trees, the thick bark is soft and springy to the touch.

▲A cool, foggy, rainy climate suits coastal redwood conifers, among the world's tallest trees. These redwoods grow near the Pacific coast in the American states of California and Oregon.

POLAR CLIMATES

Imagine living where night lasts for months. Imagine a day that lasts for months as well. The year is like that in parts of the world's far north and far south. These polar regions surround the north and south poles. The Arctic, the northern polar region, is sea surrounded by land. Its chilly Arctic Ocean is almost shut off from other oceans by northern North America and Asia. The Antarctic, the southern polar region, is mainly land surrounded by sea. Most of the land is Antarctica, a continent mainly buried by ice several kilometres deep in places. It is the coldest place on earth.

The polar winter
For half the year the north pole tilts away from the sun, and winter grips the Arctic. Meanwhile, the south pole tilts towards the sun and has its summer.

In winter at the north pole the sun does not rise for 186 days. This is the longest night on earth. With no warmth coming from the sun, Arctic lands and seas grow very cold indeed. Land and sea freeze over. Explorers can walk several hundred kilometres over sea ice from Greenland to the north pole. Little snow falls in the polar regions, but little melts either. Fierce winds stir up fallen snow, and send it whirling through the air with stinging force. These snowstorms with gale force winds are called blizzards. The world's worst blizzards happen in Antarctica, where hurricane-force winds scream down from the mountains to the sea.

►Snow covers most of Antarctica's surface. Squashed snow deep down becomes ice. An immense mass of ice covers most of Antarctica under its snow. This ice took millions of years to build up, for little snow falls in one year. Indeed Antarctica is sometimes called a frozen desert.

The polar summer
In summer at the poles the sun does not set for months, but the sun is never very high above the horizon. As a result the sun's rays travel through more air, and so are spread more widely over the ground, than rays falling on the equator. Yet summer sunshine is strong enough to melt much Arctic snow and ice. Sea ice starts breaking up. Ice islands or icebergs drift into seas outside the Arctic. Low-lying land starts thawing out. But the soil deep down stays frozen. It is known as *permafrost*.

Even in summer, Antarctica stays bitterly cold, for thick ice covers most of the land.

Life in polar climates
Only very hardy plants and animals can survive in polar climates. Few flowering plants live on Antarctica and no land animals with a backbone live there all the time. But Antarctic islands are nurseries for many thousands of seals and penguins.

Most polar plants and animals are Arctic species. Tiny trees no higher than a man's waist survive winter hidden under snow. Millions of small plants burst into bloom when the short spring leads to summer. Then, boggy pools swarm with insects. Thousands of ducks, geese, swans and wading birds fly in from farther south to nest. But the Arctic summer fades fast. The birds and their newly fledged young fly south to milder climates. Only hardy beasts like polar bears, snowy owls and the burrowing, mouse-like lemmings stay on. Somehow these survive the long, dark, Arctic winter.

Few people live all the time in polar regions. Eskimos fish and hunt seals and whales in the Arctic Ocean. Other people work on oil rigs there. Scientists man weather stations in Antarctica, but no one lives permanently on that forever frozen continent.

▲This is summer on the Alaskan tundra. Water forms boggy pools that cannot soak into the frozen soil beneath. Only low-growing plants survive the long, dark, freezing winters.

▼Ice covers polar seas in winter. The rough, greyish ice you see here is thin and mushy. The smoother, whiter areas are thicker slabs called pancake ice. When sea ice grows thicker still and spreads, no ordinary ship can force its way through.

►Photographs showing the 'Midnight Sun' seen at midsummer in the Arctic. The evening sun sinks as it seems to move from left to right across the sky. At midnight the sun reaches its lowest point. Yet even now the sun has not set. Soon it starts rising again. At midsummer, sunshine lasts longer at the poles than anywhere else on earth.

▲Zebras and gnus graze on a hot plain below Mt Kilimanjaro in Tanzania. This peak stands near the equator yet snow crowns it all the year. Kilimanjaro is Africa's highest peak and the air on top is too thin to trap heat from the sun, even though this shines down strongly.

MOUNTAIN CLIMATES

Each summer ski-lifts and cable-cars whisk thousands of tourists to the tops of mountains. Maybe you have made a trip like this. If so, you might agree with the saying that 'mountains make their own weather'.

Below the mountain the sun probably shone hotly from a blue sky. But as you rose you probably came to very different weather. First the air grew cool, then cold and windy. Perhaps thick, clammy fog

closed in, and then it rained or snowed. On the other hand, fog may have covered the lower slopes while the top was in bright sunshine. If you climbed very high indeed you might have gasped for breath.

These changes happen as you climb many mountains. Breathing grows more difficult because the air pressure decreases and thins out the higher you climb. The higher you rise above sea level, the lower the temperature falls. On average, it drops by 0.6°C for every 100 m of altitude (3.5°F for every 1000 ft), although it varies from day to day. Even in summer the highest mountain peaks are very cold indeed. Snow and ice grip high summits even in the hottest regions of the world. Near polar regions, even low mountains always wear some snow.

▶Snow and frost grip cold Alpine mountain tops all through the year. But trees grow and people build homes in the milder valleys below.

Mountain winds
High peaks are windy as well as cold. This is because high-level winds are strong and because winds hit the peaks without first being slowed down by any other ground. At 600 m (2000 ft) above sea level wind often blows three times faster than across the surface below. Hurricane force winds blowing at over 160 km per hour (100 mph) sometimes

blast high summits like Mt Everest's.

Winds crossing certain mountain ranges have been given special names. The Chinook is a warm wind that often blows east across the Rocky Mountains in winter and spring. The wind warms as it descends and melts any snow lying on the plains. When the Chinook begins to blow, temperatures may rise by 20°C (36°F) in a few minutes. The Föhn wind is a similar wind that blows across the European Alps. This wind melts winter snow and sets off the huge snow slides called avalanches.

Mountains even make winds of their own. By day, air rises as the sun's heat warms a mountainside. Then winds blow up valleys to replace the rising air. These are called *anabatic winds* and are usually light. At night, air is cooled, becomes denser and rolls down the mountain slopes. These are called *katabatic winds* and can be very strong.

Cloud and rain

The fog that often hangs on mountain slopes is really cloud. This forms as warm, moist air blows up a mountainside, then cools, until the moisture in the air condenses. But often the fog is part of a larger mass of cloud that formed elsewhere.

In places, moist winds blow in from the sea, then rise to cross a range of mountains. The rising air sheds enormous loads of rain upon sea-facing slopes. Yet if the winds shed all their moisture, the mountains' inland slopes may be dry, barren deserts.

Mountain life

As you climb a mountain near the equator you find that tropical plants give way to kinds normally found in colder climates. High peaks everywhere are homes only to plants able to survive strong winds and cold, thin air. Many of these plants form little cushions clinging tightly to the ground. Plants like edelweiss have hairs that prevent their leaves from being dried out by the wind.

Wild mountain animals include agile goats, sheep and goat-antelopes. Hooves that grip like climbing boots help them to leap sure-footedly from rock to rock, among the precipices.

▼Low cloud forms mist and fog that cling to the slopes of mountains. Scenes like this are common in the Cantabrian mountains of northern Spain.

WEATHER AT WORK

▶The heaps in this Norwegian mountain lake are stones fallen from the cliffs above. Frost prised off bits of solid rock. These pieces tumbled down and pulled up into loose slopes called scree.

INTRODUCTION

Weather has shaped and continues slowly to shape all land above sea level. This shaping starts when weather breaks up solid rock lying on or just below the surface. Geographers call this kind of break-up *weathering*.

However hard they seem, all rocks have weaknesses that weather can attack. Some rocks, such as limestone, dissolve very slowly in rainwater. Some, for example granite, have cracks that heat or cold can spilt open. Other rocks like chalk and sandstone have billions of tiny pores that let in rain. Certain rocks are easily destroyed because they are soft.

Freeze–thaw attack
In climates where temperatures fall below freezing, frost, dew and fallen rain can split rocks. First, the water trickles into cracks and fills them up. Then the water freezes and expands. The ice presses hard against the rock on each side of the crack and widens it. On high peaks, water in the rocks may freeze at night and melt by day many times each year. So flakes of stone break off layered rocks, and boulders split apart. Frost-shattered flakes of rock cover many of the world's high mountain slopes.

Swelling and shrinking
In hot deserts, cool nights and scorching days do much to break up rock. By day the surfaces of rocks become so hot they expand. By night they cool and contract, or shrink. But rock below the surface never grows as hot or cold as rock above, so does not expand or contract so strongly. This difference between the rock on the inside and outside of a boulder makes flakes split off at dusk, sometimes with quite loud cracking noises. Expanding and contracting also widens cracks and breaks a big rock mass into many smaller chunks over a period of many thousands of years.

How rock dissolves
Rain wears away some rocks in several ways. The water makes certain mineral ingredients swell up inside their rocks.

This makes the rocks break down. Water attacks feldspar, a mineral in the hard rock, granite. Feldspar slowly changes into a powdery white clay called kaolin. The other minerals in granite then fall out as scattered grains of sand. Also the oxygen that rain picks up from air combines with iron in certain rocks to form a reddish crumbly 'rust'.

Limestone is probably the rock that suffers most from the immediate effects of rain. Rain picks up carbon dioxide gas from the air. This makes rain into very weak carbonic acid. Carbonic acid dissolves calcium carbonate, the main ingredient in limestone rocks.

Mountain limestone is the limestone worst affected. Cracks already criss-cross mountain limestone, so a limestone mountain is a mass of huge, closely-fitting blocks with crevices between. Rain trickling through a crevice dissolves the rock on either side. So crevices grow wider. A mountain limestone surface may look like rows of pavements, with narrow gutters in between. As rain sinks deep down through such limestone cracks it widens them. Whole streams plunge down deep so-called swallowholes and disappear.

Far underground, the flowing water dissolves rock, leaving limestone caves.

The underground water is rich in calcium carbonate dissolved from limestone rock. But water evaporating as it drips from cave roofs leaves some calcium carbonate behind. Over many thousands of years this forms the shiny, spiky stalactites that hang from the roofs of many limestone caves. Dripping water evaporating after it hits the ground also builds the stalagmites that stick up from the dry floors of many limestone caves. Again they take a very long time to form.

▲Hot days and cool nights helped break down these rocks in the Sahara Desert. Changing temperatures split a mass of solid rock into sections. The sections broke into boulders. Then these disintegrated into stones and finally into grains of sand.

THE WORK OF WATER

The chief tool that wears away the surface of the land is running water. Rivers cut valleys and slowly wear away the highest mountains. The running water carries broken mountain rock down slopes towards the sea. There rivers shed their loads and these may start to build new land.

The work of upland rivers

Rivers attack land fastest where they race down steep mountain slopes. Many rivers start high up on hills and peaks. Here and there, water bubbles up from underground as springs. The springwater trickles downhill as tiny mountain streams. Fast-flowing streams pick up loose bits of weathered rock and carry them downstream. These stones knock against each other and against the rocky stream bed. This grinds the stones into ever smaller pieces of gravel, and gravel

into sand and mud. The tumbling stones also grind away and deepen the stream bedrock.

In time, each mountain stream cuts a steep-sided valley or gorge in its mountain. Here and there the stream may plunge down waterfalls. These form where the rocks are so hard that water has not worn them down as fast as it attacked the softer rocks downstream.

Tributaries – streams flowing in from either side – turn the main stream into a sizable river. The tributaries also carve countless little valleys in the mountainside. Ridges left between these valleys are called spurs. After many thousands of years, rivers and their tributaries will have worn down a mountain range into a mass of low ridges and spurs separated by a maze of broad, gently sloping valleys.

The work of lowland rivers

Instead of gnawing ever deeper into its bed, a lowland river attacks land sideways. The river chews away each bank, where its current hits it hardest. But much of the sand or mud removed from one bank piles up on the other bank where the water flows more sluggishly, and sheds some of its load of sand and mud. So the river swings from side to side in huge loops called meanders. As each meander works its way downstream it lops off spurs that jut into the valley from its sides. So meanders broaden and flatten the valley floor.

At last some rivers wear down all but the very lowest hills, and flow across a huge, low river plain. These broad, slow-flowing rivers carry only tiny lightweight particles of clay and silt. This load they shed into the sea.

Yet that need not be the end of the land that rivers have worn down and washed away. In sheltered, shallow, coastal waters the silt may pile up until it builds new land. Rivers like the Mississippi, Nile and Niger all reach the sea through low silt plains that they have built far out from the mainland. These plains are mostly shaped like giant fans or triangles. We call them deltas after △ (delta), the triangular fourth letter of the Greek alphabet.

►This is one end of Loch Ness, a long, narrow lake that fills a deep, narrow trench that crosses Scotland. In time, even deep lakes fill with mud brought in by rivers. Then a flat valley floor takes the place of water.

▼This beach is largely made of tiny fragments of land that a river has washed out into a shallow sea. What you see could be the broken-down remains of hills or even mountains.

◀Muddy water carries particles of rock that the San Juan River has loosened from its bed. Over millions of years this river has scoured away enough rock to dig a deep gorge through a desert. The San Juan joins the Colorado River. That river's Grand Canyon is the largest gorge on earth.

▼This aircraft pilot's view shows part of the mighty River Amazon and some tributary streams that feed it. This is the world's largest river. It snakes across a vast flat plain and carries huge amounts of mud down to the sea.

THE WORK OF ICE

Long ago, northern lands became intensely cold. Thick sheets of ice sprawled over much of North America and northern Europe. Long tongues of ice crept far down mountain valleys in the European Alps and Rockies.

This Ice Age lasted hundreds of thousands of years. By 10,000 years ago most of the ice had melted, but it left the land much changed. Moving ice had scraped away whole mountainsides and dumped them on low plains. This work still goes on in mountain ranges like the Himalayas, Alps and northern Rockies, and beneath the thick ice sheets that cover much of Greenland and Antarctica.

How ice attacks the land

Ice rivers called glaciers slowly gnaw away at rocks on many of the world's high mountains. Most glaciers begin high up on mountainsides. A glacier is born when snow fills a hollow. The weight of snow above squashes snow below and this slowly turns to ice. In time, pressure forces a tongue of ice to poke out from the hollow and start to creep downhill. This tongue is the beginning of a glacier.

The glacier grinds its way down through a valley already carved out by a river. Other glaciers flow in from smaller valleys at the sides. The sides and bottom of each glacier pick up stones and chunks of broken rock. These rasp away more rocks from the valley floor and sides. In this way a glacier chops off ridges jutting into its valley, making it wide and very deep.

Meanwhile, melting and freezing crumbles the rocks around the hollow where a glacier began. So the hollow grows larger and eats into the mountain crest behind. Beyond that crest another hollow may be growing. In time both almost meet. Only a sharp ridge is left to separate them. If three hollows gnaw back into a mountain, they carve its peak into a pyramid. The famous Matterhorn on the borders of Switzerland and Italy was shaped this way.

Debris dumped by ice

In cold climates, glaciers flow downhill until they reach the sea. Then chunks of ice snap off from each glacier's lower end or snout. These chunks float on the sea as icebergs.

In warmer climates, a glacier's snout may creep no more than halfway down a mountain before it melts. There, stones drop out, like coal arriving at the end of a conveyor belt. The fallen stones pile up into a heap known as an end moraine. Sometimes an end moraine becomes a dam that pens back water from a melting glacier. Such dams produced the long, narrow finger lakes of New York State, England's Lake District and some Alpine valleys.

Meltwater flowing from a glacier or an ice sheet can spread gravels, sands and tiny particles of ground-up rock called rock flour. Layers of clay, sand and gravel left behind by melting ice sheets cover much of northern Germany, Scandinavia, and northern parts of the United States. They are called alluvial plains.

Here and there lie mighty boulders carried great distances on moving sheets of ice before these melted. In this way

▼Alaska's Capps Glacier carved a deep, broad valley. Then, as the climate warmed up, rocks, stones and ground-up rock fell from the melting snout and piled up across the valley floor to form a mighty end moraine.

◄The towering ice cliffs at the tip or snout of the Moreno glacier as it flows down from the Argentinian Andes. Although there are deciduous woodlands close by, the presence of so much ice throughout the year has a marked cooling effect on the surrounding land.

►This is the Aletsch Glacier in the European Alps. The dark strips are moraines – loose stones and rocks fallen from mountain slopes into the slowly moving ice. Side strips are lateral moraines. Where a second glacier joins the first, lateral moraines are forced into the middle as central moraines.

►This loose mass of stones and ground-up rock fell from the glacier whose melting snout lies in the foreground of this photograph.

granite rocks from southern Scotland reached south-east Ireland. In America boulders of a hard rock called red jasper occur in Kentucky, 1000 km (600 miles) from their starting point in Canada.

WIND AT WORK

In deserts, winds attack rocks, grinding them into gravel, sand and dust. Winds carry away these particles and drop them elsewhere.

How wind attacks the land
Maybe you have felt wind-driven sand sting your ankles on a beach. Winds rarely lift sand very high, but they can hurl it with tremendous cutting power at objects in its path. This can happen in deserts.

In places the desert floor is littered with stones broken from the rocks by weathering. When winds blow hard they pick up gravel and hurl it at the bases of the nearby rocks. Bits of gravel that strike other stones or rocks may break up into grains of sand. Sandstorms hurl billions of sand grains waist high. This windblown sand smooths, polishes and rubs away the solid rock. Whizzing sand grains gnaw away the bottoms of

boulders and leave the tops perched on narrow stalks, like the caps of giant mushrooms.

Sand also digs furrows in upended layers of soft rock. Hard rock layers in between stay standing upright. This forms the strange stone desert corridors called yardangs.

Wind does more than help to wear down desert hills: it carries off the broken fragments. This leaves parts of certain deserts as low, flat plains of solid, barren rock. But wind-whipped sand attacks these too, and scoops out deep depressions. The Sahara Desert's Qattara Depression is almost as large as Wales. Part of this gigantic basin has been scraped out to below sea level.

Wind the builder
Wind drops the sand it carries, if objects block its path or the wind grows weaker. If a wind blows steadily from one direction, billions of sand grains build shifting hillocks known as dunes. Dunes come in several types.

Barkhans are dunes shaped like new moons, when seen from above. The wind pushes their sides forward until they jut out like a new moon's pointed 'horns'. Some barkhans are as high as a building of several storeys. As wind blows sand across its top, a barkhan creeps across the desert at up to 15 m (50 ft) a year.

If the wind shifts, barkhans might link up as rows of long seif dunes with sharp, wavy ridges. These dunes reminded desert peoples of swords with wavy blades: *seif* is Arabic for 'sword'. Some seif dunes in Algeria and Iran grow higher than most skyscraper office blocks.

In contrast to these sandhills, smooth sheets of sand cover some desert surfaces. Here the sand has spread out among pebbles which slowed the wind and made it shed its sandy load.

Wind carries dust particles much higher and farther than it carries grains of sand. The dust might come from rocks rubbed into powder by desert winds or ground to powder by old ice sheets. Today, thick layers of windblown dust cover much of northern China, the Midwest of the United States and Europe between France and Russia.

▲The bare, arid landscape of the Gobi Desert in Mongolia is largely due to the wind. The dry top soil is carried by the wind to northern China where it has built up into hills.

▶Wind carves rocks into strange shapes in Utah's Goblin Valley. Its solid sandstone surface has broken up, leaving hard sandstone boulders perched on softer rock.

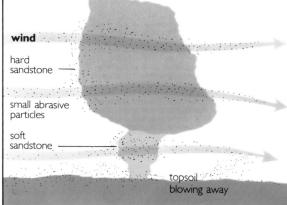

wind
hard sandstone
small abrasive particles
soft sandstone
topsoil blowing away

◀This diagram shows how wind shaped one of Goblin Valley's 'mushroom' rocks. Windblown sand grains rubbed away soft rock faster than they wore away the harder rock on top.

▲Bryce Canyon, Utah, is famous for hundreds of strange stone spires. These are remains of a great thickness of layered rock. The rest has crumbled away under the attack of wind and water.

▶Strong winds heaped up these sands at El Golea in the Sahara Desert. The dunes took many years to build. But each day the wind may change the ripple pattern on the sandy surface.

GLOSSARY

Anabatic wind Winds that blow up mountain valleys to replace warm rising air. They are usually light winds.

Anemometer Instrument used by meteorologists to measure wind speed and direction.

Anticyclone Region of high pressure in the atmosphere around which winds blow clockwise in the northern hemisphere and counterclockwise in the southern hemisphere. Anticyclones often bring fine, settled weather.

Atmosphere The gases that surround the earth.

► Orbiting space stations, such as Skylab 4, can supply meteorologists with an immense amount of new information about the earth's weather as they relay data back from high above the earth.

Barograph Meteorological instrument that records the rise and fall of atmospheric pressure by drawing a line on paper.

Barometer Meteorological instrument for measuring atmospheric pressure.

Cirrus Clouds composed entirely of ice crystals with a feathery appearance.

Cold front Edge of a cold air mass adjacent to and under a warm air mass.

Condense To reduce a gas or vapour to a liquid. When water vapour condenses, water droplets form.

Cumuliform Clouds formed by convection that look heaped or piled up.

Cyclone Region of low pressure in the atmosphere around which winds blow in a counterclockwise direction in the northern hemisphere and in a clockwise direction in the southern hemisphere. Usually associated with bad weather and strong winds.

Depression Another term for a cyclone.

Dew point The temperature at which cooling air becomes saturated and dew forms.

Evaporate Turn from moisture to water vapour.

Flash flood A sudden severe flood after a heavy downpour of rain.

Freezing fog Forms when it is foggy and the temperature falls below freezing.

Hoar frost Ice crystals that form when water vapour turns directly to ice and become attached to grass, trees and bushes.

Hygrograph Meteorological instrument for measuring humidity.

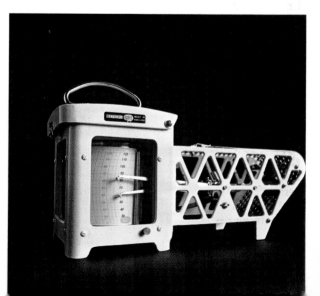

Inferior mirage Mirage that appears below the object it represents.

Katabatic wind Wind that blows down mountain slopes, caused by the cooling of air. Such winds are occasionally strong.

Meteorologist Scientist who studies the weather.

Meteorology Study of the earth's atmosphere, especially in relation to weather forecasting.

Mirage Optical illusion caused by the bending of light. Objects appear to be where they are not.

Permafrost The soil in polar regions which never thaws.

Polar front Zone where the cold air masses from the polar regions meet the warm air masses from the tropics.

Primary rainbow The brightest rainbow in the sky when there are two or more.

Radiation Giving off heat or energy.

Rime Type of frost formed during freezing fog.

Saturated The point at which a substance can absorb nothing more.

Stevenson screen A special protective container in which meteorologists keep thermometers for outdoor temperature readings.

Stratiform Clouds with a layered appearance.

Superior mirage Mirage that appears above the object it represents.

Thermograph Meteorological instrument measuring temperature.

Trade wind Wind blowing from the tropical high-pressure belts towards equatorial regions of low pressure, from north-east in the northern hemisphere and south-east in the southern hemisphere.

Troposphere The low layer of the earth's atmosphere which contains the world's weather systems.

Warm front The edge of a warm air mass advancing against a colder air mass.

Water vapour Water when it is in the form of a gas.

Weathering The breaking up of rocks as a result of the action of the weather.

◀A combined hygrograph and thermograph measures and records air temperature and moisture on a chart on a revolving drum.

▶The great fissured limestone pavement in Yorkshire, England, provides a sheltered habitat for plants.

INDEX

Acknowledgments
Ardea, Australian News
and Information Bureau,
Ian Beames, Beken of
Cowes, Black Star,
Camera Press, by
permission of the
Controller of Her
Majesty's Stationery
Office, Daily Telegraph
Colour Library, CM
Dixon, E Duffey, Werner
Forman Archive, Bob
Gibbons Photography,
Ken Hoy, ICP, Archivio
IGDA, The Image Bank,
Keystone, Magnum/John
Hillelson Agency,
NASA, NOAA, CE
Ostman/JR Simon,
Peters, Phedon/Saloyu,
Photri, Pictor,
Picturepoint, Harry
Smith Horticultural
Photographic Collection,
Spectrum Colour
Library, Brian Spooner,
Carol Unkenholz, John
Watney.